Christmas 1982

To Eveleen

From Mary + Don

The Perfect
SUNDAY LUNCH

To Anthony and Rosie Cheetham,
my publishers, for making this
their very first major cookbook

The Perfect
SUNDAY LUNCH

MARY BERRY

C

CENTURY PUBLISHING
LONDON

First published in Great Britain in 1982 by
Century Publishing Co. Ltd, 76 Old Compton Street,
London W1V 5PA

ISBN 0 7126 0040 X

Photoset by Rowland Phototypesetting Ltd
Bury St Edmunds, Suffolk
Printed in Great Britain by
Butler & Tanner Ltd, Frome and London

Contents

Acknowledgements

Firstly, my very warmest thanks go to Clare Blunt, for her help in testing and developing the recipes in this book and for typing the manuscript. To her, her 'family home-tasters', Kate and Timothy, and my own children Thomas, William and Annabel, go my sincere appreciation of their honesty, patience, and staunch support in times of crisis: their tastes are naturally reflected in this book. I would also like to thank Debbie Woolhead, a student in her final year at Sheffield Polytechnic, for coming to help me test recipes in my own kitchen, and Anne Dare, Head of Consumer Information at British Meat, for kindly agreeing to check those all-important roasting charts with her own latest research. And finally, a thank-you to Joy Langridge, my editor on the project, for her enthusiasm on a subject close to her heart . . .

The publishers would like to thank British Meat, British Turkeys and British Chicken for their kind co-operation in supplying photographs for this book.

Designed by Grub Street, London

Introduction

Sunday in our house is a special day. It is often the only day in our week when the family can get together and catch up with each other's comings and goings, share our news and compare notes on the week's activities. And though Sunday, too, can be an action-packed day, we tend to do the things we enjoy, rather than the hundred and one tasks that have to be done in the general running of the household.

And there's one thing we all look forward to – our Sunday lunch. Yes, even me. After long practice, I am firmly of the opinion that there is absolutely no need for the cook to spend the entire morning in the kitchen. With a little forethought and the minimum of organisation, cooking the Sunday lunch can be a delight instead of a chore – even for those who don't particularly find that cooking is among their *very* favourite things.

To me, there's nothing more satisfying than providing a meal that family and friends enjoy, for although it's quickly eaten, their obvious appreciation is a pleasure in itself. Not that my family approve wholeheartedly of everything I cook, but I soon learn what they *do* like, and they are kind enough to ask me to serve it again and again.

I love cooking – in that, I am lucky I admit, so let me share some of my favourite recipes with you. None is very complicated. All can be tackled by those who for one reason or another are cooking for themselves for the first time, and I have tried to cater for every kind of lunch – from the traditional roast to the 'pub-style' quiche and salad to eat outdoors on a summer's day.

There are casseroles and stews for those whose lunch must cook while they are elsewhere – at church, or visiting friends or relatives – or for those whose cooking facilities are limited. There's a curry or two for people who like a Sunday lunch with a difference, some of our tried and tested barbecue and picnic menus, and enough hot and cold puddings to keep you going for almost a year! And of course, there's the most important family lunch of the year – Christmas, with those time-honoured recipes that never fail to please. (Even the left-overs are lovely . . .) So here's to sharing our Sunday lunch. With a little practice, it can be perfect.

Mary Berry
Penn,
Bucks.

Appetizers

Appetizers need not be daunting. In fact, in my opinion, there's really no need to serve one at all for most family meals – even a Sunday lunch. In our house, we go straight to the main course, making sure there's room for one of our favourite puddings afterwards. However, there are occasions when it is nice to start the meal with a light and savoury first course – a family celebration, perhaps, or when you've invited friends over – and for some people, Sunday lunch just isn't complete without one. My rule is to keep it simple, for there's nothing worse than giving yourself too much work in the kitchen, and choose something that contrasts in colour and texture from the main course. Here are some suggestions.

FRENCH PEA SOUP

Use lettuce which has bolted and gone to seed, or the outside leaves for this soup.

1½ oz (40 g) butter
1 onion, sliced
1 small lettuce
1 lb (450 g) frozen peas
1¼ pints (750 ml) boiling stock
1 teaspoon salt
1 teaspoon sugar
freshly ground black pepper
2 sprigs of mint
2 tablespoons single cream
1 tablespoon snipped chives

Melt the butter and add the onion to the pan, cover and cook for 5 minutes. Shred the lettuce and add to the pan with the peas, stock and seasoning. Simmer without a lid for 7 minutes, or until the peas are tender.

Cool slightly, then add the mint leaves and purée the soup in a blender or processor in two or three batches.

Rinse out the saucepan and return the soup; reheat it, then taste and check the seasoning. Turn it into a tureen, swirl in the cream and sprinkle with the snipped chives.

Serves 4

Chilled Spanish Soup

This soup improves if kept in the refrigerator overnight to allow the flavours to blend.

1½ lb (675 g) ripe tomatoes
½ onion, finely chopped
1 small green pepper, deseeded
½ cucumber, peeled and roughly chopped
1 clove garlic, crushed
2 slices white bread, crusts removed and cut in pieces
6 tablespoons corn or vegetable oil
3 tablespoons white wine vinegar
½ pint (300 ml) chicken stock
salt
freshly ground black pepper
cucumber slices, to garnish

Remove the tomato skins by dropping the tomatoes in boiling water and leaving them for about 10 seconds, until the skin starts to loosen. At once, plunge them into cold water. Slip off the skins, cut in quarters and remove all the pips and membrane. Place all the ingredients except the cucumber slices in a large bowl and mix together, then reduce to a purée in a blender or processor, in two batches.

Turn into a bowl, cover and leave in the refrigerator for several hours. Divide the soup into four bowls and garnish with cucumber slices.

Serves 4–6

Avocado and Prawn Vinaigrette

It is always worth taking time to peel the tomatoes for a special meal.

2 firm tomatoes
2 oz (50 g) peeled prawns
6 tablespoons French dressing
1 spring onion, finely chopped
2 ripe firm avocado pears
salt and freshly ground black pepper

Remove the tomato skins (see previous recipe), then halve the tomatoes and remove all the pips and membrane – use these in soups and sauces – then cut the tomato flesh into fine strips.

Place the prawns in a bowl with the French dressing and spring onion and add the tomato. Toss lightly and then cover and chill.

When required for serving, cut the avocados in half and lift out the stones. Taste the tomato and prawn mixture and, if necessary, add seasoning, then spoon into the avocados and serve.

Serves 4

French Dressing

½ clove garlic, crushed
½ teaspoon dry mustard
½ teaspoon salt
good pinch of freshly ground black pepper
1 teaspoon caster sugar
¼ pint (150 ml) corn or vegetable oil
4 to 6 tablespoons cider, or white wine, vinegar

Blend the first five ingredients together in a bowl, then gradually mix in the oil with a whisk or spoon. Stir in the vinegar, taste and adjust seasoning if necessary.

Any leftover French dressing will keep in the fridge in a screw-topped jar.

Sardine and Egg Pâté

This is quick and inexpensive – and full of flavour.

4¼ oz (112 g) can sardines in oil
4 hard-boiled eggs
¼ pint (150 ml) mayonnaise (*page 18*)
¼ pint (150 ml) double cream
salt and pepper
a few drops of Worcestershire sauce

Drain the sardines and then mash well. Mash the eggs, then place them in a bowl with the sardines and mayonnaise and mix well.

Lightly whisk the cream until thick and holding a soft peak. Fold it into the sardine and egg mixture, and add seasoning and Worcestershire sauce to taste.

Turn into a dish and leave in a cool place for several hours to chill. Serve with toast and butter.

Serves 6

BRANDY LIVER PÂTÉ

Serve this with fresh toast and butter, or piled on small savoury biscuits for a party. (Chicken livers are one of my favourite things . . .)

3 oz (75 g) butter
1 small onion, finely chopped
8 oz (225 g) chicken livers
1 tablespoon chopped fresh parsley
salt and pepper
2 tablespoons brandy

Melt 2 oz (50 g) of the butter in a pan, add the onion and chicken livers and fry for 3 to 4 minutes. Sprinkle with parsley and seasoning and cook for a further 2 to 3 minutes. Leave to cool, then put in the blender or processer and blend until smooth, add the brandy and mix well. Taste and check the seasoning, and turn into a small dish.

Melt the remaining butter and pour over the top to seal. Chill well.

Serves 4

Chilled Melon and Grapes

If individual melons are expensive, buy one large one – the best buy for the season – and divide it into six, then top with the grapes and sauce.

3 baby melons
4 tablespoons redcurrant jelly
3 tablespoons sherry
juice of one lemon
1 lb (450 g) black grapes
lemon slices, to garnish
small fresh mint sprigs, to garnish

Cut the melons in half, scoop out all the pips and place each half in a glass dish.

Melt the jelly in a saucepan with the sherry and lemon juice over a low heat. Allow to cool.

Cut the grapes in half, remove all the pips and divide between the melons.

Pour the sauce over and chill for an hour. Garnish with lemon slices and small sprigs of mint before serving.

Serves 6

Parma Ham with Melon

Buy the ham from a good delicatessen – thinly sliced in a vacuum pack.

6 oz (175 g) Parma ham, very thinly sliced
1 small ripe melon
lemon wedges, to garnish

Arrange the ham on six plates. Cut the melon into six wedges, remove the seeds and place one on each slice of ham.

Garnish with lemon, and serve with freshly ground black pepper.

Serves 6

CHILLED CURRIED EGGS

Always a popular first course.

4 hard-boiled eggs
4 tablespoons mayonnaise
2 teaspoons lemon juice
1 tablespoon mango chutney juice
½ teaspoon curry powder
salt and pepper
a few sprigs of watercress, to garnish

Cut the eggs in half lengthwise and arrange on a serving dish or on individual dishes.

Blend together the mayonnaise, lemon juice, chutney juice, curry powder and seasoning. Spoon over the eggs and garnish with small sprigs of watercress.

Serves 4

MAYONNAISE

2 egg yolks
1 level teaspoon made mustard
1 level teaspoon salt
1 level teaspoon caster sugar
freshly ground pepper
1 tablespoon white wine, or cider, vinegar
½ pint (300 ml) corn or vegetable oil
1 tablespoon lemon juice

Stand a bowl on a damp cloth to prevent it slipping on the table.

Put yolks, mustard, salt, sugar and pepper into a bowl with the vinegar and mix well. Add the oil drop by drop, beating well with a whisk the entire time until the mixture is smooth and thick. Beat in the lemon juice.

Taste and check seasoning.

The Sunday Roast

I suppose whenever the subject of Sunday lunch is mentioned, our thoughts fly to memories of the big, roast joint of beef, pork or lamb, sitting on its carving board while father sharpens knife against steel, mother brings freshly cooked vegetables, still steaming, to the table, and the children are sent in search of the mustard, mint or apple sauce – then everyone takes turns with the gravy. Well, the roast joint still plays its part in many a household, but as meat is now so expensive, the joints we buy are a great deal smaller than they used to be, so it's doubly important to get the most from your roast. Remember that the better – and leaner – roasting cuts are more prone to shrinkage if they are cooked at a high temperature, so watch that cooking time like a hawk; every ounce is worth keeping. In fact, my friends at British Meat tell me from their researches that the average Sunday joint we buy these days weighs about 2lb (1 kg). All the more reason for making sure that it is properly cooked.

I have often heard new cooks complain that there's a lot of work in

preparing the Sunday roast, but there needn't be if you spend a little time in organising yourself before you start. Make a plan of action. Give yourself some breaks, then you'll at least be partly prepared for those myriad interruptions that are bound to happen when there are other people about – or the telephone trills just as you are about to baste the meat (though I'm not a great one for basting, but more of that later).

Prepare your vegetables the evening before, if you have time, and leave your peeled potatoes in a bowl of cold water in the refrigerator, with the greens washed and stored in a polythene bag alongside. Make your stuffings the day before, but don't stuff the meat until just before you are about to cook it. Cook your sauces beforehand and heat them up in boil-in-bags in a pan of water on top of the stove. Put out the carving board (in our house, we always carve on a wooden board with a channel in it to catch the juices), and sharpen the knife early in the day. Set the table in good time and check that salt and pepper pots are filled – and that one of the children hasn't appropriated the mustard pot . . . Place a jug of cold water or fruit juice in the refrigerator. Then you can concentrate on the cooking.

The only thing I cook at the last minute are green vegetables. (Add the cooking water with all its goodness to the gravy.) The gravy can be safely kept hot for a few minutes – and meat is always easier to carve if you let it stand and 'rest' for 10–15 minutes once it comes out of the oven. The fibres relax and the juice has a chance to redistribute itself throughout the meat. And I always like to wash up the pans before sitting down to lunch . . .

My consistent and best advice when asked how to choose good meat is to make a friend of your butcher. Don't be afraid of asking his advice as to what cuts are suitable for roasting; if he knows you are interested, he'll be happy to help, provided you don't pick a busy Saturday when the queue to his counter stretches out of the shop. If you need a special cut – say, a joint of veal for a change – give him notice and he should order it for you, but don't expect him automatically to save the fat trimmed from a joint he's boning and rolling for you – unless you tell him first that you'd like it for the gravy.

I'm lucky in that our butcher's shop is right across the road in the village where I live, but supermarkets too are often ready to listen to your requests for information and to help where they can.

Don't think that it's false economy to buy a larger joint than you can eat at one sitting. Larger joints roast very well, and there's all that delicious cold meat to eat up afterwards. Slices of cold cooked beef are lovely if heated through in a mustard sauce, or a thick white sauce with horseradish added. If it's not already sliced, you can cut it into neat chunks and curry it – do this with pork, lamb, and poultry too.

Pork is also lovely served cold. Cut leftovers into strips and serve them in mayonnaise with apple chunks sprinkled with a little lemon juice to prevent discolouration. This goes well with a mixed vegetable salad, or a mixture of diced cooked vegetables.

Lamb, too, can be reheated in slices or chunks in a thick white onion sauce with plenty of chopped parsley. Serve it with small potatoes boiled in their skins – or make it into pasties, with some sauce encased in the pastry with the meat.

Very small amounts of mixed meats – or poultry – can be chopped and bound in a well seasoned thick white, or mushroom, sauce and used to fill vol-au-vent cases. But there's one golden rule: when reheating cooked meat, always make sure it is *thoroughly heated through* before serving, then no harmful bacteria remain to cause tummy upsets.

And another of our house rules is: as soon as the meat leaves the table after carving, and once any second helpings have been served, it is wrapped in foil, or placed in a suitable container, covered, and put straight into the refrigerator. With a very small joint, buy the best cut you can afford and plan to use the fast roasting method at a higher temperature (see below). Cover the meat with foil for part of the cooking time, as this cuts down on basting (it will baste itself) and the foil helps to protect the meat from the fierce *direct* heat which can dry it out and cause shrinkage. Remember to cover it loosely, though, otherwise the meat will partly cook in its own juices and the result will be more like a braise or pot roast than a traditional roast.

I don't find it necessary to do a lot of basting, especially if the joint has a good top layer of fat, though very lean meats such as veal and some game birds, such as pheasant, benefit from having a layer of bacon or pork fat covering the top, or breast, and veal does need regular basting. I baste my pork joints, too, over the crackling at the start of cooking so that it gets nice and crisp.

And I don't favour lots of work with a trussing needle and thread. I

have a fine collection of skewers of all sizes, which I use to keep boned and rolled joints in shape, and stuffings inside meat and poultry while it cooks. All it needs is a little practice, and the skewers are removed before the meat goes to the table. No-one in my family likes to find string on their plate . . . If I need a joint trussed for a very special occasion, then my friend the butcher does it for me, and his trussing and tying is almost a work of art.

Cooking your roast

And so to cooking. Remember that in this country we like our meat well cooked, on the whole, on the brown side of pink, and that pork must always be thoroughly cooked. The times I have given are average times, for cookers do vary. If you find your meat is taking much longer to cook, or cooking faster than it should, check your oven – it is worth investing in an oven thermometer for this. There's no need these days to allow much time for the oven to come up to temperature, as today's cookers heat up quickly – and those of us with solid fuel cookers soon learn how long it takes. Thick pieces of meat take longer to cook than thin ones, so if your Sunday roast is a good, thick one, allow an extra five minutes' cooking time; if the joint is long and thin, deduct five minutes. To tell if your meat is cooked, insert a thin skewer into the thickest part of the joint. If the juices run clear, the meat should be cooked; if they are pink-tinged, continue cooking for a little while longer and test again. Bone is a good conductor of heat, and this may affect the cooking time. (If you use a meat thermometer, make sure that when inserted, it is not touching the bone, or you will not get an accurate reading.)

Beef

Most cuts nowadays, except for sirloin and rib, are sold boned and are therefore easy to carve, so there's little wastage. The finest cuts are suitable for roasting by the fast method, which simply means that the meat goes into a hotter oven and cooks in a shorter time. Fast roasting is good for topside, sirloin, fore rib and – if anyone can afford it for a *very* special occasion – fillet of beef. (Allow 12 minutes to the pound (450 g) – page 89.) Other cuts, such as silverside, brisket, thick or thin rib or thick flank, are coarser and do well roasted at a lower temperature for longer (slow roasting). The latter cuts are also very good

braised, and I have given recipes for some of these.

For fast roasting, season the outside of the meat (not the cut side) with salt and pepper, set it on a rack in your roasting tin and put it straight into a preheated oven. Roast, uncovered, at **400 F (200C) gas 6** for the following times:

	Medium	*Well-done*
2 lb (900 g) joint	1¼ hours	1 hour 40 mins
3 lb (1.4 kg) joint	1½ hours	2 hours
4 lb (1.8 kg) joint	1¾ hours	2 hours 20 mins
Joints over 4 lb (1.8 kg)	13 mins per lb (450 g)	18 mins per lb (450 g)

For slow roasting, melt a little fat or dripping in the bottom of your roasting tin and pre-heat the oven to **425F (220C) gas 7**. Season any outside fat with salt and pepper and place the meat in the tin. Roast for 15 minutes at high temperature, turning the joint so the outside browns evenly, then turn down the oven heat to **325F (160C) gas 3**. Cover the roasting tin with foil and cook for the following times:

2 lb (900 g) joint	2½ hours
3 lb (1.4 kg) joint	3 hours
4 lb (1.8 kg) joint	4 hours
Joints over 4 lb (1.8 kg)	1 hour per lb (450 g)

Yorkshire puddings will not cook at this lower temperature, so turn the oven up and cook these while the meat is resting – out of reach of family pets – on the counter. Incidentally, it is worth making double the quantity of batter for your Yorkshires and using the rest to make pancakes – or a Toad-in-the-Hole – the next day.

Pork

Pork should be well done, once bought, keep the joint in the freezer if the weather is warm and you are not going to cook it for a couple of days. Thaw it in the refrigerator overnight before cooking. Choose hand and spring, spare rib, leg, loin and bladebone for roasting. The crackling is most important: if you want it thin and crisp, as we like it, ask your butcher to score the fat deeply and thinly for you, rub it with a little oil and plenty of coarse salt to help it 'crispen'. Run a knife under the top skin and remove it in a piece, then let it cook loosely on top of the meat. This way, you don't lose any, and the joint isn't sitting on its own crackling! If it isn't done by the time the meat is ready, turn up the oven heat and finish it while the joint is resting before carving. I do mine in the top of the oven on an enamel plate.

Pork

Average roasting times at **350F (180C) gas 4:**	
2 lb (900 g) joint	1½ hours
3 lb (1.4 kg) joint	2 hours
4 lb (1.8 kg) joint	2 hours 40 mins
Joints over 4 lb (1.8 kg)	½ hour per lb (450 g)

For added flavour, rub the meat before roasting with dried sage leaves, or cook a pig's kidney with the joint and serve, sliced, with the roast meat.

Lamb
This is a very tasty, rather fatty meat. I love mine rarer than average with the outer skin pierced with the point of a very sharp knife at intervals and spiked with rosemary and garlic; or you can sprinkle the outside skin with crushed rosemary, or spread it with a lemon-flavoured butter and sprinkle with plenty of black pepper before roasting. Tuck a bunch of mint under the joint – and remember to skim the pan juices before making the gravy. If there's a lot of fat round the joint, you can strip it off before roasting when the meat is just warmed. A lamb is a very small animal and a whole leg or shoulder is an excellent buy. Most other cuts are sold boned and rolled and all are suitable for roasting except middle neck and scrag (the neck of the animal).

Lamb

Average roasting times at **350F (180C) gas 4:**	
2 lb (900 g) joint	1 hour 20 mins
3 lb (1.4 kg) joint	1 hour 40 mins
4 lb (1.8 kg) joint	2½ hours
Joints over 4 lb (1.8 kg)	25 mins per lb (450 g)

Veal
This tends to be a lean, dry meat without much natural fat, and most joints for roasting are sold boned and rolled. It takes well to a good, moist stuffing (see page 37) and the outside should be spread with butter or layered with bacon before roasting. Season, and roast veal at **400F (200C) gas 6**, allowing about 1½ hours for a 2 lb (900 kg) joint; 2 hours for a 3 lb (1.4 kg) joint and allow an extra 20 minutes per pound (450 g) for joints over this weight. Baste veal regularly during cooking, and cover the roasting tin with foil, if necessary, to prevent the meat from drying out.

Poultry
You will find detailed instructions for the turkey in the chapter on your Christmas Lunch (page 93), and a chicken also makes a popular Sunday roast. I like the fresh ones, but frozen ones are also good: allow 2 days for larger ones to thaw out in the refrigerator. Sit it on a plate to catch the juices and keep it well out of the reach of family pets, who will go unerringly for the breast meat! To give added flavour, I pop a bunch of fresh herbs inside, or spread the breast just under the skin with a rosemary, tarragon or garlic-flavoured butter (use your hands for this), layer it on top with strips of bacon.

Chicken can be 'stretched' by serving sausages with it, or by stuffing the neck end – which also helps to keep it moist. Don't forget to remove the giblets before cooking – and use them to make the gravy. Serve little birds – poussins – for a special occasion.

Poultry

Roast at **400F (200C) gas 6** for the following times:	
2½ lb (1.1 kg) bird	55 mins
3½ lb (1.6 kg) bird	1¼ hours
4 lb (1.8 kg) bird	1 hour 35 mins
5 lb (2.3 kg) bird	2 hours
6 lb (2.7 kg) bird	2¼ hours

When carving, carve the whole of one side first as the flesh keeps moister if the skin is intact.

And when serving any kind of meat, carve across the grain; give a little fat and lean (or dark and white meat in the case of poultry) with each serving.

Brisket of Beef with Lemon and Parsley Sauce

Really tender slow-roasted meat with an unusual sauce.

salt and freshly ground black pepper
2 oz (50 g) dripping
1/4 pint (150 ml) beef stock

Sauce
2 oz (50 g) butter
1 1/2 oz (40 g) flour
skimmed stock from the brisket made up to 3/4 pint (450 ml) with milk
juice and grated rind of 2 lemons
1 tablespoon caster sugar
2 tablespoons chopped fresh parsley

Heat the oven to 425F (220C) gas 7.

Season the meat well with salt and freshly ground black pepper. Melt the dripping in a casserole in the oven, then add the meat and cook, uncovered, for about 30 minutes, turning occasionally until the outside has browned

Reduce the oven to 325F (160C) gas 3, pour the stock round the meat, cover the casserole with a lid and return it to the oven for about 2 hours until the brisket is tender and clear juices run out when the meat is pierced with a skewer.

Lift the brisket out on to a serving dish and keep it warm in a low oven whilst making the sauce.

Melt the butter in a saucepan, add the flour and cook for a minute, stirring all the time. Gradually stir in the stock and milk and bring to the boil, stirring until the sauce has thickened. Remove from the heat, add the remaining ingredients, season well and pour into a sauceboat to serve with the brisket.

Serves 6

SLOW ROAST BRISKET WITH BUTTER BEANS

A good lean piece of brisket slow roasts beautifully. The middle will not be pink, but the meat will still be very tender – an economical Sunday joint.

6 oz (175 g) butter beans
2½ lb (1.1 kg) brisket, boned and rolled
1 large onion, cut in wedges
2 carrots, sliced
1 beef stock cube
¾ pint (450 ml) water
salt and freshly ground black pepper

Place the butter beans in a bowl and leave to soak overnight with cold water.

Next day, drain the butter and set the oven at 425F (220C) gas 7.

Put the brisket in a meat roasting tin and surround with the butter beans, onion and carrots.

Dissolve the stock cube in the water and pour over the vegetables. Cover with foil and cook for 30 minutes, then lower the heat to 300F (150C) gas 2, for 50 minutes per 1lb (450 g) of meat.

Turn up the heat to 400F (200C) gas 6, for the last 45 minutes' cooking time to allow roast potatoes to brown and a Yorkshire pudding to cook.

Arrange the meat on a serving dish. Season the vegetables well, then put into a warm dish with the stock and serve this with the meat. There is no need to make a gravy.

Serves 6

SAGE AND GARLIC ROAST

Thick end of belly pork is a good economical cut to roast; when served like this with a lovely cider sauce, it is quite special.

3 lb (1.3 kg) piece thick end of belly of pork, chined
2 cloves garlic, crushed
3 to 4 sprigs of fresh sage
2 large onions, together weighing about 8 oz (225 g)
salt and freshly ground black pepper
1 oz (25 g) flour
¾ pint (450 ml) cider

Preparation that can be done ahead
Take the rind off the piece of pork and cut into strips for crackling (page 24). (The butcher will always do this for you if he is not too busy.) Place the pork on a plate and spread with the crushed garlic. Lightly bruise the sage leaves and put on the pork. Cover with cling film or a plastic bag and leave in the refrigerator overnight. Remove the sage.

Set the oven at 375F (190C) gas 5.

Lay the onions in a meat roasting tin and put the pork on top, season well and then roast in the oven for one hour.

Put the crackling in a tin and place in the oven above the pork and cook for about 30 minutes or until crisp, remove and keep warm.

Pierce the thickest part of the pork with a skewer; if the juices run clear, the pork is cooked. Lift out and place on a serving dish.

Put the roasting tin with the onions in over a moderate heat and stir in the flour. Cook for about 2 minutes, stirring all the time, until the flour is a pale golden brown. Stir in the cider and bring to the boil, stirring until the sauce has thickened. Simmer for 2 to 3 minutes, then taste and check the seasoning.

Serves 6

Pork with Oranges

This is an unusual way of serving a loin of pork. Ask the butcher to skin and chine the meat for easy carving.

4 to 5 lb (1.8 to 2.3 kg) loin of pork (allow one chop per person)
3 large oranges
2 teaspoons salt
¼ teaspoon each of dried thyme, dry mustard and ground ginger
¼ pint (150 ml) clear honey
whole cloves (see method)
6 lettuce leaves from the heart

Set the oven at 350F (180C) gas 4.

Grate a teaspoonful of rind from one of the oranges before slicing it in half.

Place the meat on a rack in the baking tin. Mix together with salt, thyme, mustard, ginger and the teaspoon of grated orange rind and rub over the meat.

Roast it in the oven for 40 minutes, then baste the meat with the juice from one of the orange halves. Continue roasting for about 2½ hours, allowing 30 minutes per lb (450 g). During the last 45 minutes of the cooking time, baste the meat with the juice of an orange half mixed with the honey.

Peeling the remaining two oranges and cut each across into neat slices. Stud each slice with a clove. Wash the lettuce leaves, shake off any excess water and place an orange slice in each.

Place the joint on a serving dish and surround with the orange-filled lettuce leaves. Arrange the remaining orange slices over the meat. Drain the juices from the roasting tin into a sauceboat and hand the sauce separately.

Serve with Oven-cooked potatoes (page 55) and glazed carrots.

Serves 6

STUFFED SPARE RIB OF PORK

3 lb (1.4 kg) piece spare rib of pork, boned

Stuffing
1 oz (25 g) butter
1 onion, finely chopped
2 sticks celery, finely chopped
10 oz (285 g) can apricot halves in syrup
3 oz (75 g) fresh white breadcrumbs
1 egg, beaten
salt and freshly ground pepper

Gravy
1 oz (25 g) flour
½ pint (300 ml) stock
apricot syrup from the can

Set the oven at 350F (180C) gas 4.

For the stuffing: melt the butter in a small saucepan, add the onion and celery; cover and cook gently for 5 minutes. Drain the apricots, keeping the syrup for the gravy, then chop the fruit. Stir into the vegetables in the pan with the breadcrumbs, beaten egg and seasoning to taste. Mix thoroughly. Fill the pocket in the pork and then either tie into shape with fine string, or close the cavity with fine skewers.

Place in a roasting tin in the oven and roast for about 2 hours, or until tender. Pierce the thickest part of the joint with a skewer; if the juices run clear the meat is cooked, if they are slightly pink-tinged, continue cooking. Pork should never be undercooked.

Lift out the joint and place on a serving dish.

For the gravy: strain off most of the fat from the roasting tin, just leaving two tablespoons of the sediment. Stir in the flour and cook for 2 to 3 minutes.

Add the stock to the pan with the apricot syrup and bring to the boil, stirring until the sauce has thickened. Simmer for 3 to 4 minutes, then taste and check the seasoning. Serve in a warm sauceboat.

Serves 8

RUTLAND LAMB

A special way of serving roast lamb.

1 small leg of lamb, weighing about 4–5 lb
4 slices of cooked ham
2 cloves garlic, crushed
1 teaspoon dried rosemary
freshly ground black pepper
2 large onions, sliced
1 glass (4 fl. oz) white wine
salt

Set the oven at 350F (180C) gas 4.

Bone the leg of lamb using a sharp knife to remove the bone, but leave the shank bone in place. (Ask the butcher to do this for you if he is not too busy.)

Spread the slices of ham with the crushed garlic and sprinkle with some of the rosemary and pepper, then roll up the slices and stuff into the pocket in the lamb in place of the bone.

Arrange the onions in a large ovenproof casserole, lift the leg of lamb on top. Pour the glass of wine over, sprinkle with the remaining rosemary and season with plenty of salt and freshly ground black pepper.

Cover with a lid or piece of foil and cook in the oven for one hour, then remove the lid and lower the oven temperature to 325F (160C) gas 3 for the remaining cooking time (allowing 30 minutes per lb (450 g) and 30 minutes over).

Skim off any fat and serve the onions and juices with the meat.

Serve with Cheesy garlic potatoes (page 56).

Serves 8

STUFFED LAMB BOULANGÈRE

A deliciously different, easily carved Sunday joint. Ask the butcher to bone it without splitting the meat, so that it can be easily stuffed.

1 small leg of lamb
2 cloves garlic
1½ lb (675 g) onions
salt and pepper
½ pint (300mml) stock
little chopped parsley, to garnish

Stuffing
knob of dripping
1 large onion, finely chopped
8 oz (225 g) sausagemeat
1 tablespoon chopped fresh mixed herbs
1 tablespoon chopped fresh parsley
salt and freshly ground pepper

Set the oven at 375F (190C) gas 5.

First wipe the lamb, then make the stuffing: melt the dripping in a saucepan, add the onion and cook gently for 5 minutes until soft but not brown. Remove from the heat, add the remaining ingredients and mix thoroughly. Put the stuffing in the bone cavity of the leg and keep the open end closed with a skewer so that the stuffing stays inside.

Cut the garlic into thin slivers, take a small sharp, pointed knife and spear holes in the surface of the lamb. Press a garlic spike into each.

Cut the potatoes into thick slices and finely slice the onions and mix together. Place the lamb in the centre of a shallow ovenproof dish and arrange the onion and potato mixture around the meat. Season with salt and pepper and pour the stock over the lamb. Cover the dish with foil and roast for 30 minutes per lb (450 g) plus an extra 30 minutes.

After the first hour, remove the foil and baste the meat and vegetables. When the meat is cooked, remove the skewer, sprinkle the potatoes with parsley and serve straight from the dish.

Serves 8

Galloway Lamb

This stretches a small shoulder of lamb to serve 8 to 10 people, with a good gravy made from the lamb juices, and redcurrant jelly.

1 small shoulder of lamb, boned

Stuffing
4 oz (100 g) mushroom stalks, chopped
a knob of butter
1 onion, finely chopped
4 oz (100 g) lambs liver, cut in strips
a little fresh chopped thyme
2 oz (50 g) fresh white breadcrumbs
2 tablespoons chopped parsley
1 oz (25 g) porridge oats
1 egg, beaten
salt and freshly ground black pepper
redcurrant jelly, for serving

Preparation that can be done ahead
The lamb can be stuffed ready for roasting and kept in the refrigerator until required.

Open out the shoulder of lamb. Set the oven at 375F (190C) gas 5.

Put the mushroom stalks in a frying pan with the butter, onion and liver and cook all together for about 5 minutes, until the onion is soft but not brown and the liver is tender. Remove the pan from the heat and stir in the remaining ingredients, mixing thoroughly.

Spoon the stuffing into the shoulder of lamb and reshape it, securing the stuffing inside with fine skewers if necessary.

Weigh the joint and calculate the cooking time, allowing about 30 minutes per lb (450 g) plus an extra 30 minutes. Place in a roasting tin in the centre of the oven and roast until tender – the juices of the meat should run clear when pricked with a skewer. Place on a serving dish and serve with gravy (page 46) and a Celery, tomato and onion casserole (page 60) cooked alongside.

Serves 8

Herbed Lamb with Red Kidney Beans

The beans help to spin out the lamb and as it is boned it is easy to carve.

sprig of rosemary
sprig of thyme
3 cloves garlic, crushed
salt and freshly ground black pepper
3½ lb (1.5 kg) leg of lamb, boned
3 tablespoons corn or vegetable oil
2 onions, chopped
4 oz (100 g) streaky bacon, chopped
1 oz (25 g) flour
½ pint (300 ml) red wine
grated rind and juice of two oranges
15¼-oz (432-g) can red kidney beans

Heat the oven to 400F, 200C, gas 6.

Place the herbs, one clove of garlic, salt and pepper inside the leg of lamb. Place the lamb in a roasting tin and cook uncovered in the oven for about 30 minutes until the outside is browned.

Meanwhile heat the oil in a fireproof casserole and fry the onion and bacon for a few minutes until tender, add the garlic and stir in the flour, then gradually blend in the wine and orange rind and juice. Bring to the boil, stirring continually until the sauce has thickened and allow to boil rapidly for a few minutes.

Once the meat has browned, lift the lamb into the sauce and baste the meat with the sauce. Cover and return to the oven at 350F (180C) gas 4, for a further 2 hours until the meat is tender.

Drain the beans from the can and stir into the sauce for the last 30 minutes of the cooking time.

Serves 8

Frugal Pot Roast

This idea was given to me by a rather impecunious engineer on a radio station. I have tried it and found it delicious. It could also be done in a slow cooker if you have one.

2 good-quality breasts of lamb, boned
1¼ lb (550 g) prepared and sliced root vegetables, including onions, carrots, celery, swede, turnip or parsnips
½ teaspoon dried marjoram
salt
freshly ground black pepper
½ pint (300 ml) stock

Set oven at 300F (150C) gas 2.

Remove the skin and any excess lumps of fat from the breasts and cut across into 1-inch (2.5-cm) strips.

Put the vegetables into a roasting tin with the marjoram and plenty of seasoning and the stock.

Put the lamb strips into a non-stick frying pan and fry quickly until lightly brown, letting any excess fat run out. Lift out with a slotted spoon and place on top of the vegetables. Cover the roasting tin with a piece of foil and cook in the oven for 1¼ hours, then remove the foil and cook for a further 15 minutes, uncovered.

Serve with plain boiled potatoes to absorb the juices.

Serves 4

ROAST STUFFED VEAL

2½ to 3 lb (1.1 to 1.3 kg) boned shoulder or breast of veal
salt and pepper
1 oz (25 g) butter
juice of 1 lemon
1 oz (25 g) cornflour
¼ pint white wine
¼ pint (150 ml) stock
2 teaspoons tomato purée

Stuffing
1 oz (25 g) butter
1 onion, chopped
4 oz (100 g) mushroom stalks, chopped
3 oz (75 g) fresh white breadcrumbs
grated rind of 1 lemon
1 tablespoon chopped parsley
1 egg, beaten

Heat the oven to 400F (200C) gas 6.

Lay the veal flat and remove any excess fat; season well.

Make the stuffing: melt the butter, add the onion and cook for 5 minutes, stir in the mushroom stalks and cook for 2 minutes. Remove the pan from the heat and stir in the remaining stuffing ingredients and mix well. Stuff the veal and roll up firmly and tie with string, or close the fine skewers.

Place the veal on a piece of foil, dot with butter and pour over the lemon juice.

Seal the foil, place in a roasting tin and cook in the oven for about 2 hours, opening the foil for the last 30 minutes of the cooking time.

Place the cornflour in a small pan and stir in wine and stock.

Lift the veal on to a warm serving dish, add the juices from the meat to the saucepan with the tomato purée and place over moderate heat. Bring to the boil, stirring until the sauce has thickened, then simmer for 2 to 3 minutes. Taste and check seasoning. Pour into a gravy boat.

Serves 8

DUCKLING IN PORT AND CHERRY SAUCE

To carve a duck, use scissors and cut the duck's breast in half, starting from the neck end. Cut along the length of the breastbone, then through the backbone to split the bird in half. If you like, cut along the backbone, remove it and use it to make stock, so that you serve less bone on the plate. Cut each half of the bird in two, making a slanting cut between the ribs to separate the wing and the leg, so that you now have 4 portions.

1 oven-ready duckling weighing 4 to 5 lb (1.8–2.3 kg)
1 onion, quartered
salt

Sauce
3 tablespoons dripping and the juices from the cooked duckling
2 level tablespoons plain flour
½ pint (300 ml) giblet stock (see below)
1 small glass port
14 oz (400 g) can pitted black cherries, drained

Place the giblets in a saucepan, cover with cold water and add any seasoning and herbs to hand. Simmer for 1 hour to make stock.

Heat the oven to 350F (180C) gas 4.

Pat the duckling dry inside and out with kitchen paper and put the quartered onion inside. Prick the skin all over with a fork and sprinkle with salt. Place the duck on a grill rack in a shallow roasting tin, breast uppermost; roast for 35 minutes per lb (450 g) without basting.

For the sauce: put 3 tablespoons duckling dripping and juices into a saucepan, sprinkle in the flour and stir over a gentle heat for 1 minute. Gradually blend in ½ pint (300 ml) strained giblet stock to make a smooth sauce. Cook gently, stirring for about 2 minutes, or until thickened, then stir in the port and cherries.

Carve the duck (see above), and spoon the sauce over.

Serves 4

Duck with Orange Sauce

This is the classic way to serve duck – the orange sauce goes with it very well.

1 oven-ready duckling weighing about 4 to 5 lb (1.8–2.3 kg)
1 onion, quartered
salt
chopped parsley

Orange sauce
2 oranges
½ lemon
2 level teaspoons sugar
2 tablespoons brandy
2 level teaspoons cornflour

Heat the oven to 350F (180C) gas 4.

Pat the duckling dry inside and out with kitchen paper and put the quartered onion inside. Prick the skin all over with a fork and sprinkle with salt. Place the duck on a grill rack in a shallow roasting tin, breast uppermost. Roast for 35 minutes per lb (450 g) without basting.

Meanwhile, pare the rind from one orange and the lemon. Cut both rinds into fine strips. Squeeze the juice from the oranges and lemon. When the duck is cooked, transfer it to a hot serving dish and keep warm. Drain the fat from the juices in the roasting tin.

Place the sugar in a small saucepan and heat to a caramel, then add the juices from the duck. Blend the brandy with the cornflour, add this to the fruit juice, then stir into the saucepan. Bring to the boil, stirring all the time until the sauce has thickened, simmer for 2 minutes before stirring in the strips of orange and lemon peel. Taste the sauce and adjust the seasoning if necessary.

Carve the duck into four (see previous recipe) and serve with the orange sauce, sprinkled with chopped parsley.

Serves 4

TURKEY VEGETABLE BRAISE

I like to serve this with Oven-cooked potatoes (page 55), then I have a complete meal in the oven.

8 oz (225 g) carrots, sliced
1 parsnip, cubed
2 small onions, quartered
2½ lb (1.1 kg) frozen turkey breast with pork fat, thawed
½ pint (300 ml) chicken stock
salt and pepper
8 oz (225 g) packets frozen garden peas, thawed

Heat the oven to 350F (180C) gas 4.

Place the carrots, parsnip and onions in an ovenproof dish. Remove the outside wrapper from the turkey breast and place on top of the vegetables, pour over the stock and season well, then cook in the oven for 1¼ hours.

Remove the dish from the oven, cut off the inner wrapper, baste with the stock and then stir the peas into the vegetable mixture. Return to the oven and cook for a further 15 to 20 minutes, so that the peas are tender.

Lift the meat on to a heated serving dish and turn the vegetables and stock into another dish to serve, or spoon them around the joint for serving with Cranberry sauce (page 98).

Serves about 6

Buttered Roast Chicken

When cooked like this, you have lovely, moist buttered chicken. If you are not a garlic fan, just leave it out. When tarragon is available, it is nice used by itself.

3½ lb (1.5 kg) roasting chicken
3 oz (75 g) butter
1 to 2 tablespoons chopped fresh herbs
1 clove garlic, crushed
freshly ground black pepper
½ pint (300 ml) water
½ oz (12½ g) cornflour

Heat the oven to 350F (180C) gas 4.

Wipe the chicken inside and out and remove the giblets.

Cream the butter with the herbs, garlic and black pepper until soft.

Put your hand under the skin on the breast and gradually work so that the skin is separated from the flesh. Take the creamed butter and spread over the breast, working well down over the leg joints. Best to use your hand for this!

Put the chicken in a roasting tin with the giblets and water. Cover the breast with a piece of buttered paper and roast in the oven for 45 minutes, then remove the paper and cook for a further half hour, or until the chicken is tender. When the thickest part of the leg is pierced with a skewer the juices that run should be clear; if they are tinged with pink, cook the bird for a little longer.

Place the cornflour in a saucepan and blend to a paste with a little cold water.

Lift the chicken on to a serving dish and strain the juices into the saucepan; bring to the boil, stirring until thickened, then taste and check the seasoning. Simmer for 2 minutes, pour into a gravy boat and serve with the chicken.

Serves 6

CHICKEN MIRANDA

Several years ago, Miranda served us roast chicken with this sauce. Here is an adaption which needs no carving at table and can be made ahead. At the kitchen tasting session, it was voted the best chicken recipe of the Sunday lunch selection. I stuffed the chicken breasts with chestnut stuffing, but you could use your favourite turkey stuffing or even a smooth pork pâté with added fresh herbs. If you prefer to use dried chestnuts, see Oiseaux sans têtes (page 142). The recipe serves 8, as you can't get smaller cans of chestnuts. If using fewer chicken breasts, leftover stuffing can be frozen, then used to stuff a chicken for roasting.

Stuffing
15 oz (425 g) can chestnuts in water
3 oz (75 g) streaky bacon, chopped
1 small onion, chopped
6 oz (175 g) pork sausagemeat
salt
freshly ground black pepper

8 chicken breasts

Sauce
1 tablespoon corn or vegetable oil
2 oz (50 g) butter
1 medium onion, finely chopped
2 oz (50 g) flour
1 pint (600 ml) milk
4 tablespoons dry sherry
8 oz (225 g) mushrooms, sliced
salt
freshly ground black pepper

Preparation that can be done ahead
Prepare as far as ready for the oven; cover, put in the refrigerator and cook when required for about an hour.

First make the stuffing: drain and coarsely chop the chestnuts. Put the bacon in a non-stick frying pan over a low heat to allow the fat to run out. Add the onion, increase the heat and fry until pale brown. Remove from the heat and leave to cool, then mix with the sausagemeat, chestnuts and seasoning.

Beat out the chicken breasts. To do this, first take a medium polythene bag, divide into two pieces and sandwich the chicken breast inside the polythene. Beat with a rolling pin until you have a thin fillet like a veal escalope. Repeat with the other chicken breasts.

Divide the stuffing between the chicken breasts, roll up each one and secure with a wooden cocktail stick.

Heat the oil and half the butter in a frying pan, add the chicken rolls and fry to brown on all sides. Lift out with a slotted spoon and place the rolls in a casserole large enough to take them in a single layer.

Add the remaining butter to the pan and fry the onion until golden brown, stir in the flour and cook for a minute. Blend in the milk little by little, and bring to the boil, stirring until the sauce has thickened. Add the sherry and mushrooms, season well and pour over the chicken.

Cook in the oven at 350F (180C) gas 4, for about 40 minutes, or until the chicken is tender. Remove the cocktail sticks before serving.

Serves 8

MARINATED CHICKEN ROAST

This is a very effective way of getting flavour into a thawed frozen chicken.

3½ lb (1.5 kg) chicken, giblets removed
1 oz (25 g) butter
salt and freshly ground black pepper
1 teaspoon rosemary

Marinade
2 shallots, chopped
3 gloves garlic, crushed
4 tablespoons vegetable oil
2 tablespoons wine vinegar
2 bay leaves, broken
salt and freshly ground black pepper

Place the chicken in a large plastic bag with all the marinade ingredients. Leave in the refrigerator for two days, turning from time to time.

Heat the oven to 400F (200C) gas 6. Lift the chicken into a roasting tin and pour over the marinade. Dot with butter, season well with salt and pepper and sprinkle over the rosemary.

Cook the chicken for 1½ hours, basting occasionally. If the breast and thighs start to get too brown, cover with foil. When the chicken is cooked, clear juices should run from the thights if pierced with a skewer.

Lift the chicken on to a serving dish and serve with Garlic cream sauce, if liked (page 52). Any juices from the pan may be added to the sauce.

Serves 6

BRAISED CHICKEN WITH PEACHES

This is a nice, slightly sweet way of serving chicken.

3½ lb (1.5 kg) roasting chicken
1 oz (25 g) butter
4 rashers streaky bacon, cut in strips
1 onion chopped
15-oz (425-g) can peach halves
8 oz (225 g) garden peas
salt and pepper

Remove the giblets from the chicken and simmer in a little water to make stock.

Heat the oven to 400F (200C) gas 6.

Melt the butter in a frying pan and fry the chicken all over to a golden brown. Lift out and place in a large ovenproof casserole, add the bacon and onion to the fat remaining in the pan and fry quickly for 2 to 3 minutes, then lift out with a slotted spoon and add to the casserole.

Drain the juice from the peaches and make up to ½ pint (300 ml) with stock, pour over the chicken, cover and cook in the oven for 1 hour, basting occasionally.

Stir in the peas and peaches; season well and return to the oven for a further 15 minutes, or until the chicken is tender and the juices from the chicken thigh run clear when the flesh is pierced with a skewer.

Place the chicken on a serving dish and serve the peas and peaches with the stock in a separate dish. You will find no extra gravy or sauce is necessary.

Serves 6

ACCOMPANIMENTS TO SERVE WITH ROASTS

GRAVY

Everyone has their own idea about gravy; we like a thin gravy with the roast. I keep home-made stock in a concentrated form in the freezer, but I realise that this is often not practical. More often than not, I use a stock cube, plus the sediment from the meat tin and the jelly at the bottom of any appropriate dripping that I might have in the refrigerator. For red meat gravies, add a dash of Worcestershire sauce and a little red wine if there is some handy. For chicken or veal, you could add a little white wine; for game, try sherry and redcurrant jelly to give it a lift, then taste and adjust the seasoning before serving very hot.

For thin gravy: pour all the fat from the roasting tin, leaving only the sediment in the pan. Add ½ pint (300 ml) stock, stir well and boil for 2 to 3 minutes to reduce slightly. Add a little gravy browning, if you like, then season and serve.

For thick gravy: pour off most of the fat from the roasting tin, leaving about 2 tablespoons of the sediment. Stir in 1 level tablespoon of plain flour and blend thoroughly with the fat. Stir constantly with a wooden spoon until starting to brown and thicken. Gradually blend in ½ pint (300 ml) stock and bring to the boil. Cook for 2 to 3 minutes, stirring, and then season. If liked, add a little gravy browning before serving.

YORKSHIRE PUDDING

I am so often asked what is the secret of a perfect Yorkshire pudding. First of all, tastes are not all the same. Some people like them moist in the centre and crisp on the edges; others like them crisp all over. For me, I like them crisp all around the edges and the centre puffy and moist. The secret? A hot oven, smooth batter – and heating the tin and the fat in the oven before pouring in the batter.

4 oz (100 g) plain flour
1/4 level teaspoon salt
1 egg, beaten
1/2 pint (300 ml) milk and water mixed
a little dripping or lard

Heat the oven to 425F (220C) gas 7.

Put the flour and salt in a bowl. Make a well in the centre of the flour and blend in the egg with a little of the milk and water, using a small wire whisk to make a smooth paste. Blend in the remaining milk and water to make a batter (the mixture will be the consistency of pouring cream). Beat really well.

Place a little fat or dripping in the bottom of a shallow roasting tin or in the base of a 12-hole deep patty tin, and heat in the oven until the fat has melted and is very hot.

Remove the tin from the oven and pour in the batter. Return to the oven and cook the large Yorkshire pudding for about 30 minutes, or until well risen, crisp and golden brown; or small puddings for about 15 minutes. Serve at once, with roast beef.

Serves 4 to 6

Crisp Roast Potatoes

Oil gives the crispest potatoes. If you are roasting at a lower temperature, just cook the potatoes for longer; they will take about 1½ hours at 350F (180C) gas 4.

1½ lb (675 g) medium-sized old potatoes
oil

Heat the oven to 425F (220C) gas 7.

Peel the potatoes and, if necessary, cut into even-sized pieces. Parboil in water for 3 minutes, then drain well.

Pour the oil into a roasting tin to give a depth of ¼ inch (0.60 cm) use dripping which gives a good flavour but does not crisp so well.

Place the tin near the top of the oven until the oil or dripping is sizzling. Add the potatoes and roast, turning occasionally for about 1¼ hours, or until the potatoes are crisp and golden brown.

Serve with all roasts: beef, lamb, pork, veal and poultry.

Serves 4

Fresh Horseradish Sauce

Freshly grated home-grown horseradish is best, but grated horseradish can also be bought in glass bottles. All you need to do is add cream, vinegar and sugar for a really good home-made sauce.

¼ pint (150 ml) double cream
2 level tablespoons grated horseradish
1 teaspoon cider or wine vinegar
salt and freshly ground black pepper
a little caster sugar

Lightly whip the cream and add the horseradish. Stir in the vinegar, salt, pepper and a little sugar to taste and blend thoroughly. Turn into a small serving dish, cover with cling film or foil and chill well before serving with hot or cold roast beef and steaks.

SAGE AND ONION STUFFING

Serve with roast pork, or goose.

8 oz (225 g) onions, roughly chopped
¼ pint (150 ml) water
1 oz (25 g) butter
1 level teaspoon dried sage
4 oz (100 g) fresh white breadcrumbs
½ level teaspoon salt
freshly ground black pepper

Place the onions and water in a saucepan and bring to the boil. Simmer for 15 minutes, then drain thoroughly. Stir in the remaining ingredients and mix well. Use either to stuff pork or a goose, or place in a well-buttered ovenproof dish and dot with a little extra butter. Cook in a moderate oven for about 25 minutes, or until the top is golden brown and crisp.

Apple Sauce

You can, of course, use just stewed Bramley apples cooked to a mush with a little water and about 3 oz (75 g) sugar to the lb (450 g) apples. The way suggested below means you get a bright green apple sauce purée, and though you don't have to peel the apples you do have to sieve them when cooked! Use windfalls but cut any bruised parts out before cooking.

12 oz (350 g) Bramley apples
3 tablespoons water
juice of half a lemon
knob of butter
2 oz (50 g) granulated sugar

Quarter the apples, but do not core or peel. Put in a saucepan with the water and lemon juice; cover the pan with a tight-fitting lid and cook gently until the apples are soft. Shake the pan from time to time, then beat with a wooden spoon until well mashed down. Beat in the sugar and stir until dissolved. Sieve into a bowl, turn into a dish and serve with roast pork, duck or goose.

Mint Sauce

You must use fresh mint.

1 teacup mint leaves
2 tablespoons caster sugar
1 tablespoon boiling water
2 tablespoons vinegar

Chop the mint very finely. Place the sugar and water in a sauceboat and stir until the sugar has dissolved. Add the chopped mint and vinegar and mix well. Taste and check the flavour; if liked, add a little more sugar or vinegar.

Alternatively, put all the ingredients in a blender or processor and chop until it is as you like it.

Serves 4

White Onion Sauce

Onion sauce is delicious in winter with lamb or mutton when there is no fresh mint about.

1 oz (25 g) butter
1 onion, finely chopped
1 oz (25 g) flour
½ pint (300 ml) milk
salt
freshly ground black pepper

Melt the butter in a small saucepan, add the onion and cook gently for about 8 to 10 minutes until the onion is soft but not coloured. Stir in the flour and cook for a minute. Blend in the milk and bring to the boil, stirring until thickened. Season well, then simmer for 3 to 4 minutes. Serve very hot.

Serves 4

CUMBERLAND SAUCE

Any that is left will keep in the refrigerator for use at a later time with cold ham, bacon joints and game.

1 very small onion, finely chopped
1 large orange
1 large lemon
8 oz (225 g) redcurrant jelly
1 wine glass of port
1 teaspoon Dijon mustard
1 heaped teaspoon arrowroot
1 tablespoon wine vinegar

Put the onion in a saucepan, cover with water, bring to the boil and simmer for 2 minutes, then drain.

Using a vegetable peeler, remove the rind from the orange and lemon and shred finely. Put in a saucepan, cover with cold water, then bring to the boil and simmer for 5 minutes. Drain well.

Slowly heat the jelly in a pan with the port until melted.

Put the mustard, arrowroot and vinegar in a small basin and blend together, stir into the melted jelly in the saucepan and cook gently until the sauce has thickened slightly. Stir in the onion and shredded peel. Taste and, if liked, add a little seasoning, though usually I find that this is not necessary.

GARLIC CREAM SAUCE

½ pint (300 ml) single cream
2 cloves garlic, crushed
2 tablespoons chopped fresh chives
salt and freshly ground black pepper

Measure the cream and garlic into a small saucepan and boil for about 5 minutes until the cream thickens slightly. Remove from the heat and stir in the chives and seasoning. Pour into a warmed sauceboat and serve with chicken.

Vegetables

In this chapter, I've concentrated mostly on vegetables to serve with the Sunday Roast, and here my principle is – while the oven's on, pack it full. Root vegetables do well cooked alongside the meat, and you can roast parsnips, carrots and pumpkin as well as potatoes. Blanch them first and cook in the oven in a little butter, or braise in butter and stock in a foil-covered dish. Whole onions are delicious done this way. Cook and serve your vegetables together instead of separately. Try slicing the first courgettes and cooking them with frozen peas – and a whole platter of mixed vegetables can look lovely. Be adventurous with flavours, too. Purée potato with celeriac, or celeriac with swedes. Shred your sprouts and cook and purée them to serve with a dash of nutmeg. Green vegetables, however, are best cooked on top of the stove. I boil mine rapidly in a little water for the minimum of time with the lid off the pan, then serve them while still crunchy and full of goodness. Treat boiled lettuce like spinach, and ring the changes with sorrel from the garden. And whenever possible, I prefer to use fresh herbs to flavour my sauces.

OVEN-COOKED POTATOES

This is a very popular way of serving potatoes in our house. It is important to use even-sized potatoes.

1½ lb (675 g) new potatoes, scraped
2 oz (50 g) butter
salt and pepper
a little chopped mint, parsley or chives

Heat the oven to 375F (190C) gas 5.

Dry the potatoes and put the butter in an ovenproof dish in the oven until melted, then add the potatoes and roll in the butter and season well. Cover with a piece of foil and cook in the oven for one hour, shaking the dish occasionally until the potatoes are evenly coated with butter.

Remove the foil lid and continue cooking for a further 30 minutes, or until the potatoes are tender. Turn into a warm serving dish and pour over any butter left in the dish. Sprinkle with chopped mint, parsley or chives.

Serves 4 to 6

CHEESY GARLIC POTATOES

These are also delicious with cold meat or a simple grilled meat dish such as chops.

1 lb (450 g) potatoes, thinly sliced
1 fat clove garlic, crushed
salt, pepper and a little grated nutmeg
1 oz (25 g) grated cheese
1 small egg
½ pint (300 ml) milk
½ oz (12½ g) butter
a little extra grated cheese

Heat the oven to 375F (190C) gas 5. Butter an ovenproof dish.

Spread the dish with the crushed clove of garlic.

Place the potatoes in layers in the dish, seasoning well between each layer with salt, pepper and nutmeg and adding a little grated cheese.

Beat the egg in a small bowl, put the milk in a saucepan and bring to the boil, then remove from the heat and pour on to the egg. Whisk until well blended. Pour this mixture over the potatoes, dot with butter and sprinkle with the extra grated cheese.

Bake in the oven for about 45 minutes or until the potatoes are tender.

Serves 4

Hash Brown Potatoes

A crisp way of serving potatoes, very good with most grills.

2 lb (900 g) large potatoes
½ level teaspoon salt
freshly ground black pepper
1 onion, finely chopped
2 oz (50 g) pork dripping

Scrub the potatoes and boil in salted water for 10 minutes, or until the point of a knife can be inserted into the potato to a depth of about 1 inch (2.5 cm) before meeting resistance. Drain and cool, then peel and leave in a cool place overnight – or chill for several hours.

Grate the potatoes coarsely into a bowl, add the seasoning and onion and mix very well.

Melt half the dripping in a non-stick frying pan and add the grated potato, flattening with a fish slice. Cook very slowly over a low heat for 20 minutes, when the base will be golden brown. Turn out on to a large plate.

Melt the remaining dripping in the pan, then slide the potato cake off the plate and back into the pan to brown the second side slowly as before.

Turn out on to a warm dish and serve.

Serves 4 to 6

Potato and Carrot Cake

This is a very handy way of cooking vegetables alongside a joint. If you cook the vegetables in a cake tin, try turning them out and cutting them just like a cake. You can also cook them in an ovenproof casserole that will fit alongside the meat tin and serve them straight from the dish.

2 oz (50 g) butter melted
2 lb (900 g) old potatoes, sliced
1 lb (450 g) carrots, sliced
salt
freshly ground black pepper

Brush the sides of an 8-inch (20-cm) round cake tin or a small ovenproof casserole with butter. Arrange alternate layers of sliced potato and carrot in the casserole, pouring over a little melted butter and seasoning well between each layer. Press the vegetables down firmly and then cover with a piece of foil or a lid and bake in the oven at 375F (190C) gas 5, for about 1½ hours. If the oven is on a slightly lower temperature, just increase the cooking time slightly.

Run a knife around the edge of the tin and then turn the cake out on to a warm serving dish.

Serves 8

OVEN-BAKED CARROTS AND CELERY

Carrots and celery make a good combination and can be cooked in the oven alongside the Sunday joint – or a mid-week casserole.

½ head celery, sliced
1 lb (450 g) carrots, sliced
½ pint (300 ml) stock or water
1 oz (25 g) butter
salt and pepper
chopped parsley

Heat the oven to 350F (180C) gas 4, or cook the vegetables at whatever temperature the oven is set at, adjusting the cooking time accordingly. Put all the ingredients, except the parsley, in an ovenproof dish, cover with a tight-fitting lid and cook for about 1½ hours, or until the vegetables are tender. Drain if liked.

Sprinkle with chopped parsley before serving.

Serves 4 to 6

CELERY, TOMATO AND ONION CASSEROLE

This is another delicious combination of vegetables that can be cooked in the oven at the same time as the Sunday joint. Nothing could be simpler!

Once again, the cooking time can be adjusted; if your joint is cooked at a low setting, just increase the cooking time. Allow about 1½ hours in a moderate oven.

½ head of celery, sliced
14 oz (397 g) can peeled tomatoes, drained
2 onions, chopped
a teaspoon freshly chopped marjoram
lots of salt and freshly ground black pepper

Place all the ingredients in an ovenproof casserole, cover with a piece of foil or a tight-fitting lid and cook in the oven alongside the joint, until the vegetables are tender. Serve straight from the casserole.

Serves 4 to 6

GARDENER'S SELECTION

Choose any available root vegetables, taking care not to add too much swede or parsnip because of their dominant flavours.

a bag of prepared mixed root vegetables or:
8 oz (225 g) potatoes, cubed
4 oz (100 g) carrot, cubed
4 sticks celery, sliced
4 oz (100 g) swede, cubed
small parsnip, cubed
salt

Sauce
2 oz (50 g) butter
1 oz (25 g) flour
½ pint (300 ml) milk
¼ pint (150 ml) single cream
salt and freshly ground black pepper
small bunch fresh chives, finely snipped

Heat the oven to 325F (160C) gas 3. Well butter an ovenproof dish.

Cook the vegetables together in boiling salted water until barely tender – for about 5 minutes. Drain well and place in the dish.

Melt the butter in a small saucepan and stir in the flour and cook for a minute, without colouring. Gradually add the milk, stirring all the time, and bring it to the boil, stirring until the sauce has thickened. Remove from the heat and stir in the cream and seasoning to taste.

Pour the sauce over the vegetables and bake in the oven for about 45 minutes, or until the vegetables are tender. Remove from the oven, sprinkle with chives and serve.

Serves 4 to 6

QUICK-FRIED OKRA

Okra are sometimes called Ladies' Fingers and take only a short time to cook. If you only have a few, mix them with cooked peas.

12 oz (350 g) okra
butter for frying

Wash the okra pods and cut off the stems. Cook in a small amount of boiling salted water for about 5 minutes until just tender. Drain well.

Melt the butter in a large saucepan, add the okra and fry quickly for about 2 minutes, then serve at once in a warm dish.

Serves 4

CAULIFLOWER POLONAISE

Make sure that you don't overcook the cauliflower, which is best broken into sprigs first. Serve with a main course that has a gravy or its own sauce.

1 cauliflower
1 hard-boiled egg
1 oz (25 g) butter
3 tablespoons fresh white breadcrumbs
salt
freshly ground black pepper

Remove all the tough outside leaves and hard stalk from the cauliflower and break into small sprigs. Cook in boiling salted water for about 5 to 8 minutes until just tender, drain well. Keep warm in a heated serving dish.

Finely chop the egg.

Heat the butter in a frying pan until lightly browned. Remove from the heat and stir in the breadcrumbs and chopped egg. Season well, spoon over the cauliflower and serve.

Serves 4

BUTTERED JERUSALEM ARTICHOKES

Do not be put off buying these knobbly tubers because they look difficult to peel! They are delicious and peeling is made very simple by boiling them in their skins for 5 minutes first – then the skins will easily come off.

1 lb (450 g) Jerusalem artichokes
1 level tablespoon salt
2 oz (50 g) butter

Heat the oven to 350F (180C) gas 4.

Wash the artichokes and cook in boiling salted water for about 8 minutes. Drain and cool in cold water, and the skins will now peel off easily. Cut the artichokes into thick slices.

Put the butter in an ovenproof dish and put in the oven until melted, then add the artichoke slices and turn them so that they are well coated with butter.

Bake in the oven for 40 minutes until really tender, and serve with the butter in the dish.

Serves 4

JERUSALEM ARTICHOKES IN PARSLEY SAUCE

Another way of serving these good vegetables – in a sauce with either chopped parsley or chives.

1 lb (450 g) Jerusalem artichokes, washed

Sauce
1 oz (25 g) butter
1 oz (25 g) flour
½ pint (300 ml) milk
salt and freshly ground black pepper
3 tablespoons chopped parsley or chives

Put the artichokes in a saucepan of salted water, cover with a lid and bring to the boil. Simmer for about 8 minutes until the skins peel away easily. Lift out with a slotted spoon, place in a colander and run under cold water for a moment until cool enough to handle. Peel off the skins, slice the artichokes thickly and return them to the pan. Continue cooking for a little longer until the artichokes are just tender; drain well.

Meanwhile make the sauce: melt the butter in a small saucepan, add the flour and cook for a minute, stirring all the time. Gradually add the milk, then return to the heat and cook, stirring continuously, until thick. Season well and add the parsley or chives.

Place the artichokes in a warm serving dish, pour over the sauce and serve.

Serves 4 to 6

BEETROOT IN WHITE SAUCE

Many people think of beetroot as a salad vegetable, but it is delicious cooked and served hot with a white sauce. Don't worry if the sauce turns pink, as beetroot lose a lot of their colour in cooking.

1 lb (450 g) uncooked beetroot

Sauce
1 oz (25 g) butter
1 oz (25 g) flour
3/4 pint (450 ml) milk
salt and freshly ground pepper

Scrub the beetroot and leave the leaves on, then cook in boiling salted water until tender. This can take up to an hour, but will depend on the size of the beetroot. When cooked, the skins will slide off easily. Drain and peel.

Now make the sauce: melt the butter in a saucepan, add the flour and cook for a minute, stirring all the time. Add the milk and bring to the boil, stirring until the sauce has thickened; simmer for 2 minutes and season well.

Cut the beetroot into slices and place in a warm serving dish. Pour over the sauce and serve at once.

Serves 4

RED CABBAGE

One of the best, most warming vegetables, always very popular. Ideal with meat dishes, and particularly good with joints of pork or ham.

1 medium red cabbage
1 lb (450 g) windfall apples, weight after peeling
¼ pint (150 ml) water
1½ oz (40 g) brown sugar
1 teaspoon salt
4 cloves
6 tablespoons vinegar
2 oz (50 g) butter
1 tablespoon redcurrant jelly

Trim and clean the cabbage and shred very finely. Core and slice the apples.

Place the cabbage and apples in a pan with the water, sugar, salt and cloves. Cover and simmer until tender, about 45 minutes.

Remove the cloves, add vinegar, butter and jelly. Blend well over the heat, so that the butter melts and the jelly dissolves.

Taste and check seasoning, and serve in a warm dish.

Serves 4 to 6

Savoury Vegetable Rice

A mixture of rice and vegetables makes a good accompaniment to many main dishes. This recipe will serve 6 good portions, but it is easily adapted to serve more if you have a large party.

2 tablespoons oil
2 onions, chopped
12 oz (350 g) long-grain rice
1¾ pints (1 litre) chicken stock
salt
4 oz (100 g) button mushrooms, sliced
1 red pepper, seeded and cut in strips
4 oz (100 g) cooked or canned sweetcorn, drained
freshly ground black pepper
snipped chives

Heat the oil in a large saucepan, add the onions and cook gently for 5 minutes until soft but not brown. Stir in the rice and fry until the oil has been absorbed. Stir in the stock and salt, bring to the boil, then reduce the heat and simmer for 15 minutes.

Stir in the mushrooms and red pepper and continue cooking for a further 10 minutes, or until the rice has absorbed all the stock and is light and fluffy. Lightly fork through the sweetcorn and then add plenty of freshly ground black pepper. Taste and check seasoning.

Pile into a warm serving dish and sprinkle with the snipped chives.

Serves 6

Lettuce and Celery Salad

This is ideal to serve with cold meats, a meat loaf, or any rich meat dish instead of vegetables.

2 lettuce
2 celery heads

Dressing
1 level teaspoon Dijon mustard
½ teaspoon salt
1 level teaspoon caster sugar
3 tablespoons tarragon vinegar
⅛ pint (75 ml) corn oil
a little single cream (optional)

Take the outside leaves off the lettuce and cut the hearts in four. Wash in cold water. Use the outside leaves for a soup.

Take the outside sticks off the celery and keep on one side to use in casseroles or a soup. Cut the inside sticks of celery into 1 inch (2.5 cm) pieces.

Put the lettuce and celery into a salad bowl.

Blend all the dressing ingredients together in a small bowl and pour over the salad just before serving.

Serves 8

APPLE AND PINEAPPLE SALAD

This goes well with cold tongue and ham for a summer Sunday lunch.

2 tablespoons mayonnaise (page 18)
2 tablespoons French dressing (page 13)
½ teaspoon Dijon mustard
2 dessert apples, cored and sliced
½ fresh pineapple, peeled, cored and chopped
8 oz (225 g) firm white cabbage, finely shredded

Place the mayonnaise, French dressing and mustard in a large bowl and stir until blended.

Add the fruit and cabbage and toss in the dressing until evenly coated.

Turn into a serving dish, cover with cling film and chill for about an hour before serving, to allow the flavours to blend.

Serves 6 with other salads

Summer Barbecues & Picnics

Despite our uncertain climate, it's fun to plan a summer barbecue or picnic out of doors, when the family can take off to enjoy a fine day by the sea or in the countryside. The secret, I have found, is to be flexible – and find out first what the children would like to eat. Barbecues are not difficult to organise as long as you allow enough time for the coals to kindle, then settle down to an even glow – though there can be a problem in keeping food hot. My answer is to cheat a little and start off the cooking in the house first. Don't have too many courses; have plenty of simple 'back-up' food – warm crusty rolls, double-length sausages, if your butcher makes these, or cobs of corn, halved and cooked in foil with a little butter, served in the foil for the children to nibble while waiting for the rest of the food to cook.

On a practical note, plan to have sufficient table-area for serving as well as cooking, put out the salads and dips in large bowls, have lots

of kitchen paper for sticky fingers – and provide a really large bin to *keep the garden tidy*. And if it rains, don't worry. Some of my best barbecues have been held in the garage – with the doors wide open, of course . . .

A picnic, too, makes a fine Sunday lunch and it can be quite a grand affair. It's the most important meal of the family's week, after all, so serve it in style. If you know in advance where you are going, see if there's a handy wall to use as a table or serving area; take along food in those rigid plastic insulated boxes which keep cool drinks cool and hot food hot. Again, don't think in terms of elaborate food: have lots of crusty French bread and masses of simple – but different – fillings; let people choose their own. Take the Sunday joint already carved and tomatoes neatly wrapped in slices, so there's much less work to do 'on site'. Have a hot soup to serve in mugs if the weather looks doubtful – and take prepared garnishes along. It's surprising what a difference a twist of lemon or sprig of parsley can make to even the humblest sandwich.

It's nice to have a special dessert – I have often served individual mousses in those clear plastic glasses; or keep to the seasons and take along fruit – a big bowl of cherries, or melon for the children, though to my mind, there's nothing to beat strawberries and cream . . . Resist the temptation to take chocolate biscuits – they'll stick together whatever the weather and one last point – *don't* forget the salt and pepper!

Big American Beefburgers

These are lean beefburgers that are best cooked until crisp and brown on the outside and still pink in the centre. This way they will be beautifully moist and will hardly shrink at all. Cook them on the barbecue if you are eating out of doors. They taste good in warm split baps with a portion of crisp fried onions, or serve with a spoonful of simple tomato sauce (page 74).

1 lb (450 g) chuck steak, minced
1 small onion, very finely chopped
1 level teaspoon salt
freshly ground black pepper
1 tablespoon chopped mixed fresh herbs
1 egg, beaten
2 teaspoons Worcestershire sauce

Place all the ingredients together in a large bowl and mix very thoroughly.

With lightly floured hands, divide the mixture into four and shape into large flat beefburgers about 4 inches (10 cm) in diameter.

Cook them either on an oiled grid on a barbecue, over a moderate heat for about 10 minutes – turning once; or fry gently in a frying pan in a little oil or dripping. Increase the cooking time a little if necessary.

Makes 4

SIMPLE TOMATO SAUCE

A nice, simple sauce that's very good with barbecued food.

1 tablespoon oil
1 onion, chopped
1 large clove garlic, crushed
14-oz (397-g) can peeled tomatoes, drained
salt and freshly ground black pepper
a good pinch mixed dried herbs
¼ pint (150 ml) stock

Heat the oil in a small frying pan and fry the onion and garlic for 5 minutes until a pale golden brown. Add all the remaining ingredients and bring to the boil, stirring. Simmer the sauce gently for about 10 minutes until it has reduced slightly and has thickened. Taste, check seasoning and serve hot.

LAMBURGERS

These make a nice change from the more usual beefburgers. Minced shoulder of lamb is ideal.

1 onion, finely chopped
1 oz (25 g) butter
1 lb (450 g) lean minced lamb
1 finely chopped stick celery
1 tablespoon tomato purée
1 tablespoon tomato ketchup
1 teaspoon mixed herbs
salt and pepper
2 oz (50 g) fresh white breadcrumbs

Baste
1 teaspoon chilli powder
1 teaspoon celery salt
2 tablespoons soft brown sugar
2 tablespoons wine vinegar
2 tablespoons Worcestershire sauce
3 tablespoons tomato ketchup
4 or 5 tablespoons stock
a few drops Tabasco sauce

Fry the onion in the butter for about 5 minutes or until soft, then mix with all the remaining ingredients except the baste. Divide the mixture into eight equal pieces and shape into burgers.

Preheat the barbecue and oil a burger mesh, if you have one, or oil the grill.

Blend together all the ingredients for the baste and brush over the lamburgers. Grill over a moderate barbecue for about 15 minutes, turning once.

Makes 8

CHINESE PORK KEBABS

Pork fillet is quite delicious cooked this way. Leave to marinate for as long as possible.

2 tablespoons soy sauce
1 teaspoon sugar
2 tablespoons sherry
3 tablespoons water
1 lb (450 g) pork fillet
4 small onions, quartered

Blend the soy sauce, sugar, sherry and water together.

Cut the pork fillet into a neat 1-inch (2.5-cm) cubes and put in a dish with the soy sauce mixture. Cover and leave to marinate in a cool place for several hours.

Preheat the barbecue and oil the grill.

Thread the meat, alternating with quarters of onion, on four long oiled skewers and grill over a medium barbecue for about 15 minutes, turning and basting with the marinade during cooking.

These are good served with a Savoury vegetable rice (see page 68).

Makes 4

MARINATED LAMB OR CHICKEN KEBABS

Using chicken meat makes a nice change from the more traditional lamb. Onions and blanched green peppers are also good kebab ingredients. Serve with Red Devil sauce (page 80).

1 lb (450 g) lean lamb or chicken meat
4 tomatoes, quartered
16 button mushrooms

Marinade
2 tablespoons oil
1 tablespoon wine vinegar
1 clove garlic, crushed
salt
freshly ground black pepper

Preparation that can be done ahead
Prepare the lamb or chicken and leave in the marinade until required.

Cut the meat into neat 1-inch (2.5-cm) cubes. Blend all the marinade ingredients together and pour over the meat in a bowl, cover and leave to marinate for several hours or – better still – overnight.

Heat the grill to hot, or use a barbecue if you have one.

Oil four long skewers and thread on the pieces of meat, tomatoes and mushrooms alternately. Season lightly and then put under the grill for about 10 minutes, turning frequently until the meat is tender. Put on a warm dish and serve with plain boiled rice, Red Devil sauce and a crisp green salad.

Serves 4

SPICY CHICKEN DRUMSTICKS

These drumsticks have a sticky sauce, so they are best cooked under a grill and then taken outside to eat. Provide plenty of paper napkins or kitchen paper.

8 chicken drumsticks
salt and freshly ground pepper

Sauce
1 rounded tablespoon apricot jam
1 tablespoon Worcestershire sauce
3 tablespoons tomato ketchup
1 tablespoon soy sauce
1 level teaspoon Dijon mustard
pinch cayenne pepper
1 large clove garlic, crushed

Heat the grill to moderate and blend all the sauce ingredients together very thoroughly.

Season the drumsticks and brush over the sauce. Oil the grill rack and lay the drumsticks on it. Grill for about 20 minutes, turning regularly and brushing with more sauce during cooking. The time will vary with the size and thickness of the drumsticks, but the chicken is cooked if the thickest part of the drumstick is pierced with a skewer and the juices come out clear. If they are pink, continue cooking for a little longer.

Enough for 8 drumsticks

Greek Meatballs

Serve these with your favourite Barbecue sauce, or try the Red Devil sauce on page 80.

1 lb (450 g) lean minced lamb
2 oz (50 g) semolina
3 tablespoons Worcestershire sauce
1 level teaspoon salt
1/4 teaspoon dried marjoram
freshly ground black pepper
1 to 2 cloves garlic, crushed

Preheat the barbecue and brush the grill with oil.

Mix all the ingredients together in a bowl and then knead to a firm mixture.

Using wet hands, shape the mixture into small balls about 1 inch (1.25 cm) in diameter. It should make about 25 to 30 meatballs.

Lightly oil long metal skewers and thread on the meatballs. Grill over a medium barbecue for about 10 minutes, brushing with a little oil during the cooking and turning the skewers. They should be crispy brown on the outside.

Makes 25 to 30

RED DEVIL SAUCE

A good spicy sauce to serve with barbecued food such as sausages, grilled chops, meatballs or chicken joints.

14-oz (397-g) can peeled tomatoes
2 teaspoons sugar
2 cloves garlic, crushed
2 tablespoons oil
2 tablespoons wine vinegar
1 tablespoon Worcestershire sauce
1 tablespoon tomato ketchup
salt
freshly ground black pepper
1 teaspoon Dijon mustard

Place the contents of the can of tomatoes in a saucepan and cook to a pulp over a moderate heat, stirring occasionally. This should take about 10 minutes.

Remove the pan from the heat and stir in the rest of the ingredients. Purée in a blender or processor until smooth, then return to the pan and reheat before serving. Taste and check seasoning.

Serves 4

LAMB NOISETTES

If the barbecue is crowded – or it is raining outside – these are also very good grilled.

6-cutlet piece best end of neck of lamb
salt and pepper
a little dried rosemary
3 lambs kidneys

Preheat the barbecue and oil the grill.

Ask the butcher to bone the best end of neck for you. Alternatively, it is simple to do it yourself: cut off the chine bone at the thick end of the joint and trim away all the excess fat from the meat. Using a sharp-pointed knife, cut along either side of each bone and ease it out.

Season the meat well and sprinkle with rosemary. Remove the skin and cores from the kidneys and lay along the width of the meat. Roll up lengthwise and tie firmly at 1-inch (1.25-cm) intervals with fine string. Cut the joint into 6 even slices, securing each slice with two fine skewers to make sure that the kidney will not pop out during cooking.

Grill over a moderate barbecue for about 10 to 15 minutes, turning once, until the juices run clear.

Makes 6

FRESH SARDINES

These make a nice change from the more usual barbecue fare.

Preheat the barbecue and oil the grill.

Choose large fresh sardines and clean thoroughly, leaving the heads and tails on. Well coat the sardines in a Beleine sea salt. This is not strong-tasting, and gives the sardines a lovely crisp coating.

Cook over a medium barbecue for 8 to 10 minutes, turning frequently.

Serve with wedges of lemon and a good dressed salad.

TROUT

Trout baked in foil are very good for a barbecue and make another nice change from the usual meaty food.

4 fresh trout
butter
foil
salt
freshly ground black pepper
4 slices of lemon

Preheat the barbecue.

Clean the trout, leaving the heads and tails on. Wipe dry and lay each fish on a square of buttered foil. Season well, place a small knob of butter inside each fish and lay a slice of lemon on top.

Close the foil carefully at the sides and ends to seal in the juices whilst cooking. Place on the barbecue and cook over a moderate barbecue for 25 minutes, turning occasionally.

Serve the trout from the foil with all the juices poured over.

Serves 4

QUICK LEMON HOLLANDAISE

3 egg yolks
2 teaspoons wine vinegar
2 teaspoons lemon juice
4 oz (100 g) unsalted butter
1/4 teaspoon salt
pinch of white pepper

Put the egg yolks in a blender with the vinegar and lemon juice and blend on maximum speed for a few seconds.

Just before serving, bring the butter to boiling point in a small saucepan, switch the blender to maximum speed for a few seconds and then slowly pour on the boiling butter; blend until thick, add seasoning and pour into a warmed sauceboat. Serve at once.

Serves 6

Be Your Own Pizza Pie Factory

Pizzas with generous toppings and a fresh salad make a delicious lunch for a crowd – inexpensive too! I made these four for sixteen mixed adults and children; their appetites were healthy, especially those of the five boys amongst us. If you want to make these ahead, you can par-bake them for half the cooking time early in the day, then finish them off just before serving.

The dough made with 3 lb (1.3 kg) of flour was divided into four and made four 10-inch (25-cm) pizzas. You will need four large baking trays; if you don't have four, make rectangular pizzas in roasting tins or large Swiss roll tins. If you only want to make one, I suggest you use a Scone dough made from 12 oz (350 g) self-raising flour, 1 teaspoon baking powder, 3 oz (75 g) butter and about 8 fl oz (200 ml) milk.

The grown-ups drank quantities of red plonk with the pizzas. The children had 'Shirley Temples', copying the *Pizza Pie* restaurant: lemonade, plus Grenadine, with bendy straws and slices of fruit in the glass. The older boys had ice-cold weak shandies.

Dough
a large 3.31 lb (1.5 kg) bag of strong flour
5 teaspoons salt
2 sachets Harvest Gold Easy-blend dried yeast
1 tablespoon sugar
1½ pints (900) ml) warm water
2 tablespoons oil
extra oil for brushing later

General tomato base
2 tablespoons oil
3 large onions, chopped
3 large 14-oz (397-g) cans peeled tomatoes
14-oz (397-g) can tomato purée
3 cloves garlic, crushed
2 teaspoons sugar
salt and pepper

Bacon and mushroom topping
3 tablespoons oil
8 oz (225 g) button mushrooms, sliced
16 thin rashers streaky bacon
salt and pepper

Sausage topping
1 lb (450 g) pork sausagemeat

Traditional Italian topping
6 oz (175 g) Gruyère cheese, grated
a small can of anchovies
about 30 black olives, stoned

Cheese, tomato and green pepper topping
6 oz (175 g) mature Cheddar cheese, grated
1 small green pepper, seeded and chopped

First make the dough: measure the dry ingredients into a large bowl – a clean washing-up bowl will do. Add water and oil and work to a firm dough. Knead on a floured surface, then return the dough to the bowl. Cover with a plastic bag or cling film and leave to rise in a warm place until doubled in bulk. While this is happening, prepare the toppings.

For the general tomato base: heat the oil in a saucepan, add the onion and fry until soft. Add the remaining ingredients and cook without a lid until the mixture is thick and pulpy. Taste and check seasoning and, if you like, add a few fresh chopped herbs.

For the bacon and mushroom topping: measure the oil into a frying pan and fry the mushrooms briskly for 1 minute, turning. Remove the rind from the bacon.

For the sausage topping: flatten the sausagemeat out in a large non-stick pan to a round about 9-inches (22.5-cm) in diameter to form a cake. Fry on both sides until brown and cooked through – this will take about 10 minutes. It helps when turning it over to reverse it on to a plate on top of the pan, then slip the sausagemeat cake back into the pan to cook the second side.

For the Traditional Italian and Cheese, tomato and green pepper toppings, no preparation is needed; just collect the ingredients together.

To assemble: first knock back and knead the dough, then divide into four equal pieces. Flatten out each portion on floured baking trays to 10 to 11-inch (25 to 27.5-cm) rounds, or rectangles about 8 by 10 inches (20 by 25 cm). Just use whatever oven trays you have available. Brush each pizza with oil and then spread with the general tomato base, putting a little extra on the Traditional Italian dough. Now cover each with the toppings.

Bacon and mushroom topping: spread over the mushrooms and then arrange the bacon on top to make a cartwheel effect. Season.

Sausage topping: lift the sausagemeat cake on to the pizza base.

Traditional Italian topping: scatter over the cheese, then arrange the anchovies and olives on top. Season.

Cheese, tomato and green pepper topping: scatter the cheese and green pepper on the pizza and season.

Leave the pizzas to prove (rise) until puffy in a warm place for about 30 minutes. If you are not baking them all at once, put a couple in a cool place for a slower rise whilst the first two are baking.

Bake at 425F (220C) gas 7, for 20 minutes; lower the heat to 375F (190C) gas 5, for a further 20 minutes, or until the pizzas are evenly baked and pale brown at the edges. If the oven is full it may take longer.

Serve hot, sprinkling a couple of them with freshly chopped parsley or chives. I found that the children favoured the sausage and bacon ones and the grown ups like the lot!

A very large bowl of tossed salad is really all that is needed to go with the pizzas.

Bacon and Onion Quiche

Serve either hot or cold. The soured cream gives an extra sharpness.

Pastry
6 oz (175 g) plain flour
1½ oz (40 g) lard
1½ oz (40 g) margarine
about 6 teaspoons cold water

Filling
8 oz (225 g) bacon trimmings
1 onion, chopped
2 eggs, beaten
¼ pint (150 ml) single cream
¼ pint soured cream
a little salt
plenty of freshly ground black pepper

Heat the oven to 425F (220C) gas 7.

Put the flour in a bowl, add the fats – cut in small pieces – then rub in with the fingertips until the mixture resembles fine breadcrumbs. Add sufficient cold water until the mixture forms a firm dough, then roll out on a floured surface and use to line a 9-inch (22.5 cm) flan tin. Line with greaseproof paper and baking beans and bake in the oven for 10 minutes, then remove the greaseproof paper and return the flan to the oven to dry out for a further 5 minutes. Reduce the oven temperature to 350F (180C) gas 4.

Remove the rind from the bacon and cut in strips. Place in a non-stick pan with the onion and cook gently for about 10 minutes, or until the onion is soft and the fat has run from the bacon. Lift out with a slotted spoon and put in the pastry flan case.

Mix the eggs with the creams in a bowl, add a little salt (not too much if the bacon is salty) and plenty of freshly ground black pepper. Pour into the flan case and bake in the oven for about 30 minutes, until the flan is set and the top is a pale golden brown.

Serves 6

Smoked Haddock Quiche

Pastry
8 oz (225 g) plain flour
2 oz (50 g) margarine
2 oz (50 g) lard
about 3 to 4 tablespoons cold water

Filling
1 lb (450 g) smoked haddock
5 to 6 rashers streaky bacon
2 eggs
2 egg yolks
¼ pint (150 ml) milk
¼ pint (150 ml) single cream
freshly ground black pepper

Heat the oven to 425F (220C) gas 7.

First make the pastry: place the flour in a bowl, rub in the fats with the fingertips until the mixture resembles fine breadcrumbs, add the water and mix to a firm dough. Knead lightly, then roll out the pastry on a floured surface and use to line a 9 by 11-inch (22.5 by 27.5-cm) tin about 1-inch (2.5-cm) deep. Chill for about 15 minutes.

Line the tin with greaseproof paper and baking beans and bake blind for about 10 minutes until the pastry is just starting to colour at the edges, then remove the paper and beans and return the flan to the oven for 5 minutes to dry out. Reduce heat to 375F (190C) gas 5. Place the haddock in a pan with just enough water to cover and poach for about 10 minutes – until the flesh easily flakes with a fork.

Lift the fish on to a plate and flake, removing any skin and bones and then put in the base of the flan case.

Cut the bacon into thin strips across the rashers and fry until crispy and the fat has run out. Spoon over the haddock.

Put the eggs, yolks, milk, cream and black pepper in a bowl and mix well until blended. Pour over the fish, then bake for 30 to 40 minutes until set and a pale golden brown. Serve either hot or cold.

Serves 6 to 8

HAM AND EGG SLICE

Filling
1 lb (450 g) cooked ham, coarsely minced
8 oz (225 g) pork sausagemeat
freshly ground black pepper
4 hard-boiled eggs, sliced
10½ oz (298 g) can condensed consommé

Pastry
12 oz (350 g) plain flour
3 oz (75 g) hard margarine
3 oz (75 g) lard
about 4 tablespoons cold water to mix
milk or beaten egg to glaze

Heat the oven to 400F (200C) gas 6.

Place the ham, sausagemeat and black pepper in a bowl and mix well. It is not usually necessary to add salt.

For the pastry: put the flour in a bowl and rub in the fats until the mixture resembles fine breadcrumbs. Add sufficient water to mix to a firm dough. Roll out two-thirds of the pastry into a rectangle on a floured surface and use to line a 11 × 7 × 1½-inches (27.5 × 17.5 × 2.75-cm) tin.

Lay half the meat mixture in the base of the tin, then cover with a layer of hard-boiled egg slices and finally the remaining meat.

Roll out the rest of the pastry into a rectangle for the lid. Damp the edges of the pie, lay the lid on top and seal the edges well. Trim off any surplus pastry and decorate the edges. Make two slits in the centre for the steam to escape and glaze with milk or beaten egg.

Bake in the oven for 45 minutes. Gently heat the consommé. Carefully pour this into the pie through the slits in the centre. If the pie will not take all the consommé at first, you will find that the rest may be added as the pie cools.

When quite cold, leave the pie in the refrigerator overnight. Cut into slices to serve. This is ideal to take on a picnic.

Serves 8

CHICKEN AND HAM RAISED PIE

A delicious cold meat pie that is made a day ahead – ideal for a picnic or cold summer lunch in the garden.

Filling
4 lb (1.8 kg) chicken
8 oz (225 g) bacon pieces, finely minced or chopped
1 tablespoon chopped fresh mixed herbs
8 oz (225 g) pork sausagemeat
1 teaspoon ground mace
2 teaspoons salt, depending on the saltiness of the bacon
freshly ground black pepper
6 small hard-boiled eggs, shelled
beaten egg and milk to glaze

Pastry
12 oz (350 g) plain flour
1 teaspoon salt
5 oz (150 g) lard
1/4 pint (150 ml) plus 2 tablespoons water

Greasen an 8-inch (20-cm) loose-bottomed cake tin.

First carve off the leg and thigh from the chicken, then remove the skin and bone. Take off the meat from the rest of the bird, discard the skin and make stock from the bones. Cube all the chicken meat and put in a bowl with the bacon, herbs, sausagemeat and seasoning, and mix well.

Now make the pastry: put the flour and salt in a bowl. Put the lard and water in a saucepan over a moderate heat and allow the lard to melt and the water to boil. Make a well in the centre of the flour and pour on all the liquid, mixing quickly with a wooden spoon or fork until it becomes a smooth dough. When cool enough to handle, take two-thirds of the dough and put into the tin. Knead it up the sides of the tin until it stands about 3 inches (7.5 cm) from the base.

Put half the meat mixture in the tin, level it off and make six dents in the mixture. Arrange the eggs in them. Cover with the remaining mixture and flatten it off. Brush the rim of the pastry top with beaten

egg and milk. Roll out the remaining pastry to a circle just over 8 inches (20 cm) for the lid and lift on top of the pie. Press the edges firmly together and flute, using the thumb and first finger of the right hand and the index finger on the left hand, or just press into a pattern with the prongs of a fork. Make four holes in the top of the pie and decorate with pastry leaves, if liked. Brush with beaten egg and milk, and bake at 425F (220C) gas 7 for about 45 minutes. Reduce the heat to 350F (180C) gas 4, for a further 30 minutes. Remove from the oven and leave to cool in the tin. Chill the pie overnight before turning out and serving, sliced in wedges.

Serves 8 to 10

Cold Roast Fillet of Beef

And now for a little sheer luxury, very expensive – but there's no waste. Occasionally there is a reason to have such a family celebration lunch in summer. A whole fillet weighs about 3½ to 4½ lb (1.5 to 2 kg) and you will get about four servings to the lb (450 g). You need a good-sized piece for the best results. Ask the butcher to tie it with string and prepare it for you. Cook it the day before, then chill it before slicing.

To roast, first rub a little butter all over the fillet and season with salt and freshly ground black pepper.

Roast at 425F (220C) gas 7 for 12 minutes to the lb (450 g). This will give a brown outside and a pink centre.

Leave to cool, then chill.

Slice just before serving (not more than two hours ahead), and arrange attractively on a large flat dish. Garnish with small sprigs of parsley and watercress and serve with mustard and horseradish sauce.

Picnic Loaf

There is plenty of meat in this loaf as it is important to pack it tightly into the tin so that after cooking, when it will shrink a little, it may be cut into really thin slices.

5 to 6 rashers streaky bacon
12 oz (350 g) minced beef
8 oz (225 g) beef or pork sausagemeat
2 oz (50 g) fresh white or brown breadcrumbs
1 small onion, grated
1 carrot, grated
1 egg
1 teaspoon salt

Heat the oven to 350F (180C) gas 4.

Take the rind from the bacon and use to line the base and sides of a 1-lb (450-g) loaf tin.

Place all the other ingredients in a large bowl and mix together very thoroughly, so that they are evenly blended. Press the mixture tightly into the loaf tin, cover with a piece of foil and stand in a roasting tin half-filled with hot water. Bake in the oven for about 1¼ to 1½ hours. When cooked, the juices will run clear if a skewer is put in the centre of the loaf.

Remove from the oven and leave to cool. Pour off any fat, then turn out the loaf. Cover it with a piece of cling film and chill in the refrigerator for several hours.

Serve sliced with salads.

Serves 6

Christmas

Most people choose turkey for Christmas. A fresh one is certainly the best, but considerably more expensive than a frozen one and, with care, a frozen bird can taste delicious. Thaw at room temperature allowing 3 hours per lb (450 g) of turkey; a larder is the perfect place to do this, with the door shut – away from family pets! When thawed, remove the wishbone for easy carving.

For a really moist turkey breast, insert bacon under the breast skin before cooking; the bacon will naturally baste the bird during cooking. It is not difficult to lift the skin away from the breast meat. Loosen at both ends, carefully slipping the fingertips under the skin.

Serve with Chestnut stuffing which is cooked inside the body cavity of the bird, and Sausage, lemon and thyme stuffing which is best cooked in the front end of the turkey. Also serve a thin gravy made from the giblets – these can be simmered for a stock the day before. Cranberry sauce and Bread sauce are essential too.

What size turkey to buy
A 6 to 8 lb (2.7 to 3.5 kg) oven-ready turkey will give 8 to 12 servings.
A 10 to 13 lb (4.5 to 5.9 kg) oven-ready turkey will give 15 to 20 servings.
A 14 to 20 lb (6.5 to 9 kg) oven-ready turkey will give 20 to 30 servings.

Preparation of turkey for the oven
Stuff the turkey, but ideally don't do this until the day you are going to roast it, unless you can put the turkey in the refrigerator. Stuffings go off quickly in a warm kitchen. By all means make the stuffings a day ahead and wrap them in foil or transparent wrap, then store in the refrigerator. You could also freeze them for up to a month beforehand. Brush the turkey with butter, season well and wrap loosely in foil.

Roasting the turkey

Approx. weight	*Oven temperature*	*Approx. cooking time*
5 lb (2.3 kg)	350F (180C) gas 4	2½ hours
10 lb (4.5 kg)	350F (180C) gas 4	3¼ hours
15 lb (6.8 kg)	350F (180C) gas 4	4 hours
20 lb (9 kg)	325F (160C) gas 3	5 hours

Put the turkey in the oven on a shelf below the centre and roast as above. Open the foil for the last 1¼ hours of the cooking time for a large bird over 10 lb (4.5 kg) for the last 50 minutes or so or for a smaller bird. This ensures that you will get a crisp brown bird. Baste from time to time.

To tell when the turkey is done
Pierce the thickest part of the thigh with a fine skewer: if the clear juices run out, the turkey is cooked. If the juices are slightly pink-tinged, continue cooking until they are clear. After cooking, cover the turkey with foil, keep warm in the oven and allow to rest for 10 minutes before carving.

Chestnut Stuffing

This should be enough for a 14 to 16 lb (6.3 to 7.2 kg) turkey.

Buy dried chestnuts from a good delicatessen; they are easy to use and give a stuffing with lots of flavour and texture.

8 oz (225 g) dried chestnuts, soaked overnight
8 oz (225 g) streaky bacon, chopped
1 large onion, chopped
1 tablespoon sugar
1 oz (25 g) butter
1 oz (25 g) porridge oats
3 oz (75 g) fresh white breadcrumbs
1 egg, beaten
about 1 teaspoon salt
freshly ground black pepper

Rinse the chestnuts in fresh water after soaking, then put them in a saucepan. Cook them in boiling water for about 30 minutes until they are tender but slightly crisp. Drain, cool a little and peel off any remaining bits of skin. Chop them coarsely.

Put the bacon in a non-stick frying pan, let the fat run out over a low heat, then increase the heat. Add the onion and sugar and allow them to brown a little. Stir in the butter, oats, breadcrumbs and chestnuts, and bind together with the egg. Season to taste, adding more salt if necessary (this will depend on the saltiness of the bacon)). Use to stuff the body cavity of the turkey.

SAUSAGE, LEMON AND THYME STUFFING

This is a stuffing I have been making for years. It goes in every book I have written on main dishes, as I have yet to find a better one for a classic roast turkey. I do prefer to use fresh thyme and fresh parsley.

1 oz (25 g) butter
1 onion, chopped
1 lb (450 g) pork sausagemeat
4 oz (100 g) fresh white breadcrumbs
grated rind and juice of one lemon
1 level teaspoon salt
freshly ground black pepper
2 tablespoons chopped parsley
1 level teaspoon fresh chopped thyme or ½ teaspoon dried thyme

Melt the butter in a saucepan and fry the onion gently until soft, for about 10 minutes. Stir in all the remaining ingredients and mix well together. Use to stuff the breast of the turkey.

Sausages and bacon rolls
The sausages and bacon rolls can be cooked at the top of the oven, if the oven is large enough. Chipolata sausages will take about 35 minutes and the bacon rolls about 15 minutes. If space is short, do both of these quickly under the grill.

Chipolata sausages
Grill the sausages, pricking them if liked, under a medium grill, for about 10 to 15 minutes. Turn them regularly so that they are evenly brown. If you like little sausages, give the chipolatas an extra twist in the centre to make them half the size, then cut them apart.

Bacon rolls
Stretch de-rinded bacon rashers on wooden board with the back of a knife until they are almost twice their original length. Cut each rasher in half and roll up. Place on long thin skewers and grill for 6 to 8 minutes under a medium grill, turning once, until golden brown.

Roast potatoes
Roast for the last 1½ to 1¾ hours above the turkey. They take longer than usual as the oven temperature is lower. Again, if oven space is short you can do these in an electric frying pan or even a deep-fat fryer.

Rich Gravy

This may be done the day ahead.

the turkey giblets, washed
2 onions, peeled
1 bayleaf
1 sprig parsley
1 blade mace
1½ pints (900 ml) water
2 tablespoons turkey fat
1 oz (25 g) flour
salt and pepper
3 tablespoons sherry
a little gravy browning, if necessary

Put the giblets into a pan with the onions, bayleaf, parsley, mace and water. Cover, bring to the boil and simmer for 4 hours. Strain.

Put the turkey fat into a pan, blend in the flour and cook over a low heat, stirring continually, until the flour has turned brown. Add the giblet stock a little at a time, blending until smooth. Bring to the boil and simmer for 2 minutes until it has thickened. Season well with salt and pepper, stir in the sherry and add a few drops of gravy browning.

Bread Sauce

1 onion, peeled
6 peppercorns
1 bayleaf
1 pint (600 ml) milk
3 oz (75 g) fresh white breadcrumbs
salt
knob of butter

Place the onion, peppercorns and bayleaf in a saucepan with the milk and bring the milk very gently to the boil. Turn off the heat (or move the pan from an electric hob) and leave the milk to infuse for 30 minutes. Lift out the onion, peppercorns and bayleaf.

Stir in the breadcrumbs, a little salt and the knob of butter. Reheat the sauce almost to boiling point, then remove from the heat.

Cover with a piece of damp greaseproof paper pressed on top of the sauce to prevent a skin from forming, and keep warm. If the sauce becomes too thick on standing, add a little extra milk to thin it down.

Cranberry Sauce

This is a very fresh-tasting sauce as the cranberries are raw, and it has a rich, bright colour.

8 oz (225 g) cranberries
10 to 12 oz (275 to 350 g) caster sugar
grated rind and juice of one orange

Place all the ingredients in a blender or food processor and purée until smooth.

Christmas Pudding

Turn the pudding out before lunch but leave the basin on top to cover it and keep it moist. If you wish to flame the pudding, heat both the spoon and the brandy or rum, *then* pour over the pudding and set alight at once.

2 oz (50 g) self-raising flour
coffee spoon of mixed spice
12 oz (350 g) mixed dried fruit
3 oz (75 g) fresh white breadcrumbs
3 oz (75 g) shredded suet
1 oz (25 g) almonds
1 small cooking apple
1 rounded tablespoon marmalade
3 oz (75 g) grated carrot
4 oz (100 g) soft brown sugar
2 eggs, beaten

Grease a 1½ pint (900 ml) pudding basin.

Sift together the flour and mixed spice. Put the dried fruit in a large bowl with the breadcrumbs and suet. Roughly chop the almonds. Peel and coarsely grate the apple, add to the bowl with almonds, marmalade and carrot.

Stir in the spiced flour and sugar and mix well together, then stir in the eggs and mix thoroughly. Turn into the basin, cover the top with greaseproof paper and a foil lid.

Steam or boil for about 6 hours. If boiling, place on an unturned saucer in a saucepan with boiling water coming half-way up the sides of the basin. In either case, keep an eye on the water level and top up as necessary with boiling water during cooking. Lift out of the pan, leaving the greaseproof and foil in place. Cool, then cover with a fresh foil lid and store in a cool place until required.

Simmer for a further 3 hours on Christmas day.

Serves 8

Brandy or Rum Butter

3 oz (75 g) unsalted butter
6 oz (175 g) icing sugar
3 tablespoons brandy

Beat the butter until soft, then add the icing sugar and continue to beat until the mixture is light and fluffy. Beat in the brandy, then turn into a serving dish and leave in the refrigerator to harden before serving.

Take out at least an hour before serving.

Brandy Cream

Very simple and light.

Whisk ½ pint (300 ml) double cream with 4 tablespoons brandy together with 1 oz (25 g) sugar until light and fluffy.

RUM SAUCE

Some families like the old-fashioned rum sauce. We still make it, although I prefer Brandy cream or Brandy butter.

1 oz (25 g) butter
1 oz (25 g) flour
½ pint (300 ml) milk
1 oz (25 g) caster sugar
3 to 4 tablespoons rum

Melt the butter in a small pan and then blend in the flour and cook, stirring, for a minute. Add the milk a little at a time and bring to the boil, stirring until thick and smooth. Stir in the sugar and rum. Mix well and simmer for 2 minutes.

Cover the sauce with a piece of buttered moistened greaseproof paper until it is required, so that a skin does not form.

Alternatively, seal it in a boil-in-the-bag, then keep it hot in a pan of simmering water.

OLD ENGLISH TRIFLE

8 oz (225 g) can pears
6 to 8 individual bought sponge cakes, split in half
strawberry jam
1 almond macaroon
12 maraschino cherries, chopped
1 tablespoon maraschino syrup
5 tablespoons sherry
½ pint (300 ml) custard (see below)
¼ pint (150 ml) whipping cream
a few toasted slivered almonds

Drain the pears, reserving the juice, and cut the fruit into small pieces.

Sandwich the sponge cakes together with strawberry jam and place on the bottom of a shallow 2-pint (a good litre) serving dish. Cover with the pears and top with the crumbled macaroon. Sprinkle over the chopped cherries, pear juice, maraschino syrup and sherry.

Prepare the custard and allow to cool before pouring over the fruit and sponge cakes. Leave to set.

Lightly whisk the cream until thick, then spoon or pipe over the custard. Sprinkle with almonds and serve.

Serves 6 to 8

CUSTARD

3 egg yolks
1 oz (25 g) caster sugar
1 heaped teaspoon cornflour
½ pint (300ml) milk

Mix together the egg yolks, sugar and cornflour in a bowl. Warm the milk in a pan until hand-hot, then pour on to the egg yolk mixture, stirring constantly. Return the mixture to the saucepan and cook gently, stirring constantly, until the custard thickens. Do not allow it to boil or it will curdle. Let it cool, then use it for the trifle as above.

Rich Fudge

A fudge that is full of flavour and ideal to serve with truffles and coffee after Christmas lunch.

8 oz (225 g) hard margarine
1 good tablespoon golden syrup
1 lb (450 g) granulated sugar
13½-oz (383-g) can condensed milk
1 teaspoon white distilled malt vinegar
1 teaspoon vanilla essence

Put the margarine and syrup in a saucepan and let the margarine gently melt over low heat. Add the sugar, stir well and bring slowly to the boil, stirring until the sugar has dissolved. Boil gently for 5 minutes. Add the condensed milk and bring back to the boil. Boil gently for 20 minutes, stirring continuously, otherwise the fudge will stick.

Remove the pan from the heat, add the vinegar and vanilla essence and beat well until the fudge starts to thicken.

Turn into a greased 7-inch (17.5-cm) square tin and leave to set.

Cut the fudge into about 64 pieces and store in an airtight tin until required.

Makes 64 pieces

Rum Truffles

These are rich and rather good. Make and serve them for a special occasion such as Christmas with coffee. If you have no rum, use a little brandy instead.

3.5 oz (100 g) bar plain chocolate
1 egg yolk
½ oz (12½ g) butter
2 tablespoons rum
1 to 2 oz (25 to 50 g) chocolate vermicelli, or a little powdered drinking chocolate

Break the chocolate into pieces, place in a bowl and stand over a pan of gently simmering water until melted, stirring occasionally.

Remove from the heat, add the egg yolk and butter and beat well, then beat in the rum, and continue beating until the mixture is thick. Chill until firm. Divide the mixture into 12 pieces and shape each into a ball. Coat in the vermicelli or drinking chocolate powder.

Keep in a cool place until required.

Makes 12

Old English Meals

I make no apology for including some of our favourite national dishes, for no book on Sunday lunches would be complete without a recipe for Boiled Beef and Carrots, or Steak and Kidney Pudding. This is the kind of dish that has almost become an institution, and for which the visitors to our shores search high and low – only to learn that the best examples are cooked at home and served on the family table. There are one or two borrowings from overseas, too; dishes which unashamedly make the best of our high-quality home-grown ingredients – fine fish, good meat and succulent vegetables – and which we have quietly adopted for special occasions.

You will gather from all this that some of these dishes are not cheap. They call – in an old-fashioned way – for good cuts of meat – no making do with second-rate . . . So my solution would be to buy less, serve smaller portions, have heaps of good vegetables to serve with the main dish – and spin it out with a pastry crust! These are dishes which the man in the family might like to try, for statistics show that more and more men are taking over the cooking of the Sunday lunch. And there's many a good fellow who would be proud to tackle a steak and kidney pudding . . .

Boiled Beef and Carrots

Remember to warn the butcher to brine the meat for you. Ideally, let him know 10 days beforehand. It is essential to simmer the joint slowly otherwise it will shrink. Serve with the vegetables around the meat.

3½ lb (1.5 kg) boned and rolled salt silverside
1 lb (450 g) small whole onions
1 lb (450 g) small whole carrots
8 sticks celery, sliced
8 medium potatoes, halved
2 tablespoons chopped parsley

Mustard sauce
2 oz (50 g) butter
2 oz (50 g) flour
½ pint (300 ml) milk
½ pint (300 ml) stock from the beef
1 level tablespoon dry mustard
1 level tablespoon sugar
3 tablespoons vinegar
salt and pepper

Wash the meat in cold water and, if necessary, soak overnight to remove any excess salt. Place the meat in a large saucepan in plenty of water and cover with a lid or foil. Bring to the boil, then simmer very gently for 2 hours, checking to make sure there is still enough water.

Add the vegetables and continue cooking for a further hour.

Lift the meat on to a serving dish, remove the vegetables with a slotted spoon and spoon around the meat. Keep warm and, when ready to serve, sprinkle the vegetables with parsley.

To make the sauce, melt the butter in a saucepan, add the flour and cook, stirring continually, for 2 minutes. Stir in the milk and stock from the beef and bring to the boil, stirring constantly. Simmer for 2 minutes to thicken. Blend together the mustard, sugar and vinegar and stir into the sauce. Cook for one minute, then add salt and pepper. Serve with the meat.

Serves about 8–10

BOILED MUTTON WITH CAPER SAUCE

As mutton is rarely available these days, this recipe is ideal for a leg of lamb which has been in the freezer for longer than usual.

3½ lb (1.5 kg) leg of lamb
2 onions, each stuck with 3 cloves
2 carrots, sliced
3 sticks celery, sliced
juice of half a lemon
2 sprigs of thyme
1 parsley sprig
6 peppercorns
1 blade mace

Caper sauce
1½ oz (40 g) butter
1½ oz (40 g) flour
2 tablespoons capers
1–2 teaspoons vinegar from the capers
1 teaspoon prepared mustard
salt and pepper
a little sugar
2 tablespoons single cream or top of the milk

Put the mutton or lamb in a large saucepan and cover with water. Bring to the boil, removing any scum as it forms. When the water is free of scum, add the vegetables, lemon juice, thyme, parsley, peppercorns and mace. Cover the saucepan and simmer gently for 1¾ to 2 hours, allowing 25 minutes per lb (450 g).

When the lamb is nearly cooked, make the sauce: melt the butter in a saucepan and stir in the flour. Cook for a minute, stirring, then add one pint (600 ml) of the liquor from the lamb and bring to the boil, stirring constantly. Stir in the capers, vinegar, mustard and seasoning to taste, adding a little sugar. Add the cream and then pour into a warm serving dish or sauceboat. Lift out the lamb and place on a serving dish.

Serves 8

SHERRIED KIDNEY VOLS-AU-VENT

These may also be made with pig's kidney if the housekeeping is running low.

7½-oz (213-g) packet of 12 frozen vol-au-vent cases
8 lambs kidneys
1 oz (25 g) butter
salt
freshly ground black pepper
½ teaspoon chopped fresh marjoram
4 oz (100 g) button mushrooms, sliced
1 oz (25 g) flour
¼ pint (150 ml) chicken stock
2 tablespoons sherry
3 to 4 tablespoons single cream

Heat the oven to 425F (220C) gas 7, and bake the vol-au-vent cases according to the directions on the packet, for about 12 minutes. Remove them from the oven and scoop out the insides.

Meanwhile, skin the kidneys, cut each in half horizontally and snip out the cores with a pair of scissors or a sharp knife. Cut into thin slices.

Melt the butter in a large frying pan and fry the kidneys for about 5 minutes until tender. Season well with salt and pepper and the marjoram, stir in the mushrooms and cook for a further 2 to 3 minutes. Stir in the flour and cook for a minute, then blend in the stock and sherry and bring to the boil, stirring until the sauce has thickened. Taste and check seasoning and then remove from the heat and stir in the cream.

Place the cooked vol-au-vent cases on an ovenproof serving dish and divide the kidney mixture between them. Return to the oven for a further 10 minutes to heat through.

Serve with a green vegetable such as broccoli or French beans.

Serves 4 to 6

Boiled Bacon with Mustard Glaze and Peaches

Always soak collar of bacon overnight as it can be salty. Take care to simmer very slowly so that the meat is not tough.

2½ lb (1.1 kg) piece of collar of bacon
15-oz (425-g) can peach halves

Glaze
2 teaspoons dry mustard
1 tablespoon soy sauce
2 tablespoons soft brown sugar
½ teaspoon powdered ginger

Soak the bacon overnight in a bowl of cold water.

Next day, drain and place it in a saucepan, cover with cold water and bring to the boil. Cover the pan and simmer gently for 20 minutes to the lb (450 g) and 20 minutes over – about 1 hour 10 minutes. When cooked, lift out and when cool enough to handle, remove the skin and score the fat in diamond shapes.

Heat the oven to 400F (200C) gas 6.

Prepare the glaze: place the mustard, soy sauce, brown sugar and ginger in a small bowl. Drain the peaches, reserving the syrup, and put them in a small ovenproof dish. Add 3 tablespoons of the peach syrup to the glaze and mix well, then pour the remainder back over the peaches and put in the oven to heat through whilst it is coming up to temperature.

Put the bacon in an ovenproof serving dish, spoon over the glaze and cook in the oven for about 10 minutes until the glaze is shiny and bubbling. Remove from the oven and serve cut in slices with a little of the brown glaze, and a peach with some of the juice with each slice.

Serves 8

Cold Ham

Soak the joint overnight before cooking if it is likely to be salty. Always ask your butcher's advice on this. Once you have brought the joint to the boil, simmer very gently until tender, then – when slightly cooled – cover with the glaze and brown. Chill overnight and the meat will be easy to carve.

4 lb (1.8 kg) piece of corner gammon, boned and rolled
3 bay leaves
peppercorns
1 onion, sliced
cider

Glaze
3 tablespoons demerara sugar
1 tablespoon dry mustard
2 tablespoons thin honey

Use a saucepan of the same width as the bacon joint, place the gammon in it, add bay leaves, peppercorns, onion and pour over the cider to cover. If you use a pan of the correct size, you will not need too much cider to cover the meat. Bring to the boil, cover with a lid or foil and simmer gently for 20 minutes per lb (450 g) plus an extra 20 minutes. When the meat is tender, lift it carefully out of the pan and leave it until it is cool enough to handle. Peel off the skin using a small sharp knife. Score the fat in diamond shapes.

Mix together the ingredients for the glaze and spread over the ham fat. Cover the lean parts of the bacon with foil, then brown the fat in a hot oven 450F (230C) gas 8, for about 5 minutes until the glaze has turned a golden brown. Remove and leave to become quite cold, then chill overnight.

Next day, carve in thin slices and arrange on a serving dish. This is good served with a Cumberland sauce (page 52), new potatoes and a selection of salads.

Serves 12

STEAK AND KIDNEY PUDDING

1¼ lb (550 g) skirt of beef
8 oz (225 g) ox kidney
1 onion, finely chopped
3 level tablespoons plain flour
1½ level teaspoons salt; freshly ground black pepper
1 tablespoon Worcestershire sauce
scant ¼ pint (150 ml) water

Suet crust pastry
8 oz (225 g) self-raising flour
4 oz (100 g) shredded suet
1 level teaspoon salt
about 9 to 10 tablespoons water

Grease a 2½-pint (1.4-litre) pudding basin. Cut the steak and kidney into ½-inch (1.25-cm) cubes, removing any fat. Use scissors to remove the core from the kidney. Put the steak and kidney in a bowl with the onion, flour, seasoning and Worcestershire sauce. Mix together well.

To make the pastry: put the flour, suet and salt into a bowl and gradually add the water and mix to a soft but not sticky dough. Take one third of the pastry and roll out on a lightly floured surface to a circle large enough to fit the top of the basin. Roll out the remaining pastry and use to line the basin.

Fill the basin with the meat mixture and add the water. Dampen the edges of the pastry and cover with the pastry lid, pressing the edges firmly together to seal. Cover the pudding with a pleated piece of greased, greaseproof paper, then a lid of foil.

Stand the basin in a saucepan and pour boiling water into the pan until it comes halfway up the sides of the basin. Boil gently for 4 hours, or steam for 5 hours in a steamer over a pan of gently boiling water. Top up with boiling water when necessary during cooking.

When cooked, lift out the pudding and remove the foil and greaseproof paper lids. Stand the basin on a plate, wrap a napkin around it and serve the pudding at once.

Serves 6

Brisket of beef with new potatoes and broccoli. Serve it with a lemon and parsley sauce.

Above: Roast stuffed veal served with extra stuffing baked with the meat. Right: Lamb and pepper kebabs are good for barbecue picnics – or lunch indoors.

Left: Traditional roast turkey for the perfect Christmas lunch, served with cranberry sauce and bread sauce.
Above: Crispy devilled chicken pieces – multiply up the recipe to serve a crowd.

Left: A tasty lamb casserole – good for winter days. With a topping of sliced potato, it becomes a Lancashire hot pot. Above: Steak and kidney pie – a traditional English dish to prepare the day before, leaving Sunday morning free.

A hearty Pork stew with parsley and lemon dumplings makes a change for Sunday lunch.

Steak and Kidney Pie

A traditional dish which can be prepared the day before to leave Sunday morning free. It is always a great family favourite.

1 lb (450 g) skirt beef
8 oz (225 g) beef kidney
1 oz (25 g) flour
1 oz (25 g) dripping
1 large onion, chopped
½ pint (300 ml) beef stock
1 level teaspoon salt
freshly ground black pepper
4 oz (100 g) mushrooms, sliced
8-oz (227-g) packet frozen puff pastry, thawed
a little milk, to glaze

Cut the steak and kidney into cubes about 1 inch (2.5 cm) each and toss in the flour until well coated. Melt the dripping in a saucepan, add the meat and onion and cook until the meat is browned. Stir in the stock and bring to the boil, stirring all the time. Add the seasoning, then partially cover the pan and simmer for 1½ hours, or until tender. Stir in the mushrooms and continue to cook for a further half hour, or until the meat is tender. If preferred, the meat may be simmered in a slow oven for about 2 hours until tender. Taste and check seasoning.

Place a pie funnel in a 1½ pint (900 ml) pie dish and then spoon the meat around and leave to become quite cold.

Heat the oven to 425F (220C) gas 7.

Roll out the pastry on a floured surface and use to cover the pie. Seal and crimp the edges, then make a small slit in the centre to allow the stem to escape and use any trimmings to decorate the top of the pie. Brush with a little milk and cook in the oven for 30 to 35 minutes, until the pastry is well risen and golden brown and the meat is heated through.

Serve with boiled potatoes and a green vegetable or carrots.

Serves 6

Individual Fillets en Croûte

These are delicious with a quick sauce made from a couple of cartons of soured cream blended with 4 teaspoons creamed horseradish, and salt and freshly ground black pepper to taste.

six 4 to 5 oz (100 to 150 g) fillet steaks
salt and freshly ground black pepper
2 oz (50 g) butter
1 tablespoon oil
1 medium onion, chopped
4 oz (100 g) button mushrooms, sliced
1 tablespoon chopped parsley
2 oz (50 g) cooked ham, shredded
two 14 oz (397 g) packets frozen puff pastry, thawed
beaten egg, to glaze

Heat the oven to 425F (220C) gas 7.

Season the steaks well with salt and pepper. Melt the butter in a frying pan, add the oil and fry the steaks briskly for about 2 minutes on each side until the outsides are sealed and brown but the centre will still be pink. Lift out with a slotted spoon on to a plate and leave on one side.

Fry the onion in the fat remaining in the pan for about 5 minutes, or until just tender. Put in a bowl and add the mushrooms, parsley and ham and mix well.

Roll out the pastry fairly thinly on a working surface and cut into six rectangles large enough to wrap around the steaks.

Place a steak on each piece of pastry and divide the mushroom and ham mixture between them. Brush the edges of the pastry with beaten egg and then wrap over to enclose each steak in a parcel. Seal the edges and knock up with a sharp knife. Lift on to a baking sheet, glaze with more beaten egg and bake for 20 minutes, until the pastry is well risen and golden brown.

Lift on to a serving dish and serve at once.

Serves 6

CORNISH PIE

This is really a large Cornish pasty, ideal for a Sunday crowd. Serve either hot or cold.

Filling
1 lb (450 g) raw minced beef
6 oz (175 g) potatoes, finely diced
4 oz (100 g) carrots, finely diced
1 large onion, finely chopped
1½ level teaspoons salt
plenty of freshly ground black pepper

Pastry
12 oz (350 g) plain flour
3 oz (75) g) margarine
3 oz (75 g) lard
about 4 tablespoons cold water
a little milk, or beaten egg, to glaze

Heat the oven to 425F (220C) gas 7.

Place the beef, potatoes, carrot, onion, salt and pepper in a bowl and mix well.

For the pastry, put the flour in a bowl and rub in the fats until the mixture resembles fine breadcrumbs. Add enough water to mix to a firm dough. Turn on to a floured surface and roll out two-thirds of the pastry into an oblong and use to line a tin measuring 11 × 7 × 1½ inches (27.5 × 17.5 × 3.75 cm). Put the meat on the pastry and press down evenly. Roll out the remaining pastry to form a lid. Damp the edges of the pie and cover with pastry, press the edges well together. Trim off the surplus pastry and crimp the edges. Brush the top with milk or beaten egg and make two slits for the steam to escape.

Bake for 20 minutes, then reduce the heat to 350F (180C) gas 4, and cook for a further 35 to 40 minutes until pastry is browned and has shrunk slightly from the sides of the tin. Serve either hot or cold.

Serves 6 to 8

Welsh Lamb Hot Pot

Fillet of lamb makes a very good hot pot; it is ideal if your family do not enjoy taking the meat from the bones in middle neck.

1½ lb (675 g) fillet of lamb
1 tablespoon flour
8 oz (225 g) onions, sliced
8 oz (225 g) carrots, sliced
1 large cooking apple, peeled, cored and sliced
salt
freshly ground black pepper
1½ lb (675 g) potatoes, sliced
¾ pint (450 ml) hot stock
1 tablespoon tomato purée
½ teaspoon mixed dried herbs

Preparation that can be done ahead
The vegetables may be prepred ahead and left in a bowl of cold water.

Heat the oven to 350F (180C) gas 4.

Cut the lamb into slices about ¼-inch (0.60-cm) thick and coat in flour. Place in a large 4-pint (2.3-litre) ovenproof dish, cover with the onions, carrots and apple slices, seasoning well. Finally, arrange the potatoes neatly overlapping on top.

Stir the hot stock with the tomato purée and herbs, then pour over the potatoes. Cover with a lid and cook in the oven for 1½ hours, then remove the lid and continue cooking for a further 30 minutes, or until the meat and vegetables are tender.

Serves 6

LANCASHIRE HOT POT

Prepare the vegetables ahead and put in a basin of cold water. Leave overnight and assemble the dish on the day. As a change to make a straightforward casserole, add all the sliced potatoes to the hot pot 30 minutes before the end of the cooking time, put in a handful of peas – and a tablespoon of tomato purée if you are not using the kidneys.

1½ lb (675 g) potatoes, sliced
2 onions, chopped
6 to 8 carrots, sliced
3 sticks celery, sliced
2 lb (900 g) middle neck of lamb
2 lambs kidneys (optional)
a little seasoned flour
salt
freshly ground black pepper
¾ pint (450 ml) stock

Preparation that can be done ahead
If preparing the vegetables ahead, put half the potato slices in a bowl on their own to use for the top.

Heat the oven to 350F (180C) gas 4.

Wipe the lamb and cut into even-sized pieces, or your butcher may do this for you. Cut the kidneys in half and peel off the skin, snip out the core with a pair of scissors and coat both the lamb and kidneys with seasoned flour.

Arrange layers of vegetables and meat in a large ovenproof dish of at least 4-pint (2.3 litre) capacity, seasoning well between each layer and finishing with a layer of potato slices neatly arranged on top.

Pour over the stock, cover with a piece of buttered greaseproof paper and a tight-fitting lid and cook for 2 hours.

Remove the lid and paper and continue to cook, uncovered, for a further 30 minutes.

Serves 4

VENISON PIE

Venison for stewing is very lean, reasonable in price and so good. I find it best if marinated in the refrigerator for 48 hours first.

2 lb (900 g) stewing venison, cut in 1-inch (2.5-cm) cubes
½ pint (300 ml) inexpensive red wine
2 bay leaves
4 oz (100 g) streaky bacon, rind removed and chopped
1 large onion, chopped
1 oz (25 g) flour
½ pint (300 ml) stock
1 tablespoon redcurrant jelly
2 teaspoons salt
plenty of freshly ground black pepper
6 oz (175 g) button mushrooms, sliced

Pastry
6 oz (175 g) plain flour
1½ oz (40 g) lard
1½ oz (40 g) margarine
about 6 teaspoons cold water
beaten egg, to glaze

Put the venison in a glass or china bowl with the red wine and bay leaves, cover and leave to marinate in the refrigerator for about 48 hours.

Heat the oven to 350F (180C) gas 5. Strain the red wine from the venison and keep. Discard the bay leaves.

Put the bacon in a frying pan and cook over a gentle heat until the fat begins to run out; lift on to a plate with a slotted spoon. Add the onion to the fat remaining in the pan and fry gently until tender. Stir in the flour and cook for a minute, then gradually blend in the stock and reserved wine. Bring the liquid to the boil, stirring continuously until the sauce has thickened. Stir in the venison with the redcurrant jelly and seasoning, and the bacon pieces. Transfer to a large ovenproof casserole, cover and cook in the oven for 2½ hours, or until the venison is tender.

Add the mushrooms for the last 10 minutes of the cooking time. Remove from the oven and allow to cool, then put the contents of the casserole in a 2½-pint (1.4 litre) pie dish.

Increase the oven temperature to 400F (200C) gas 6.

For the pastry: put the flour in a bowl, add the fats cut in small pieces and rub in with the fingertips until the mixture resembles fine breadcrumbs. Add enough water to bind to a firm dough. Roll out the pastry on a floured surface and use to cover the pie. Glaze with a little beaten egg and bake for about 30 minutes, until the pastry is golden brown and the meat heated through.

Serves 6

JUGGED HARE

Hares are reasonably priced and a good buy when in season, from August to March.

1 oz (25 g) butter
3 tablespoons corn or vegetable oil
1 hare, skinned, cleaned and jointed
2 onions
6 cloves
¼ pint (150 ml) port
1 tablespoon lemon juice
½ pint (300 ml) stock
2 sticks celery, chopped
2 tablespoons redcurrant jelly
1 teaspoon salt
freshly ground black pepper
2 oz (50 g) butter and 2 oz (50 g) flour creamed together

Forcemeat balls
2 oz (50 g) bacon, chopped
2 oz (50 g) shredded suet
2 tablespoons chopped parsley
grated rind of one lemon
½ teaspoon fresh thyme
4 oz (100 g) fresh white breadcrumbs
1 egg
salt and pepper
oil or butter for frying

Heat the oven to 350F (180C) gas 4.

Melt the butter and oil in a large frying pan and fry the joints of hare a few at a time for about 10 minutes each, until well browned. Arrange the joints in a large ovenproof dish or casserole.

Pierce the onions with the cloves and put them in the dish with the hare. Now add the port, lemon juice, stock, celery, redcurrant jelly, salt and plenty of black pepper. Cover the dish with a lid and cook in the oven for about 3 hours until just tender.

About 30 minutes before serving, stir the creamed butter and flour into the liquid in the casserole to thicken it. Return to the oven for the remaining cooking time.

Meanwhile, prepare the forcemeat balls: place all the ingredients in a bowl, season well and mix until the mixture is loosely bound together. Shape the mixture into about 12 balls and fry in a little oil and butter until crispy brown on all sides. Add to the casserole just before serving.

Serves 6

KOULIBIAC OF SALMON

Not exactly Old English! But it must be included for a super Sunday lunch with a difference.

Either buy a 2 lb (900 g) salmon or a 2 lb (900 g) pink-fleshed trout, which is cheaper and just as good for this recipe.

Clean the fish and cover with cold water, add a tablespoon of salt and a couple of bay leaves. Cover the pan, bring the water slowly to the boil and simmer for one minute.

Remove from the heat, cool for about an hour in the water, then lift out and remove the head, skin and bone. The remaining fish will weigh about 1 lb (450 g).

Serve the Koulibiac with a sauce made by blending a couple of cartons of soured cream with seasoning and snipped chives, or with a quick Hollandaise sauce (page 83).

about 1 lb (450 g) cooked fresh salmon or pink trout, flaked
4 oz (100 g) long-grain rice
2 oz (50 g) butter
1 onion, chopped
3 oz (75 g) button mushrooms, sliced
2 tablespoons chopped parsley
2 hard-boiled eggs, sliced
juice of half a lemon
1½ teaspoons salt
freshly ground black pepper
14 oz (397 g) packet puff pastry, thawed
a little beaten egg, to glaze

Heat the oven to 425F (220C) gas 7.

Cook the rice as directed on the packet until just tender, then drain and rinse well. Put into a large mixing bowl.

Melt the butter in a frying pan and fry the onion gently until transparent but not coloured, add the mushrooms and fry for a further minute until just tender. Stir the onion and mushrooms into the rice with the parsley, eggs, lemon juice, salt and pepper and mix thoroughly, then carefully fold in the flaked fish.

Roll out one-third of the pastry on a floured surface to a rectangle 14 by 9 inches (35 by 22.5 cm) and lift on to a large baking tray. Spoon the filling along the centre of the pastry, leaving a border of pastry around it. The finished Koulibiac should be tall and narrow.

Now roll out the remaining pastry to cover the entire Koulibiac. Brush the border with beaten egg and lift the pastry over the top of the filling. Seal the edges together using a fork, then neaten with a sharp knife, leaving about ½ inch (1 cm) rim of pastry all the way round. Use any trimmings to make leaves and decorate the top. Glaze this with beaten egg and bake for about 20 minutes until well risen and golden brown.

Transfer to a warm serving dish for serving.

Serves 8

SPECIAL FISH PIE

A great standby for Sunday lunch for a crowd; use any white fish such as cod, haddock or whiting or even monkfish, if you can get it.

12 oz (350 g) white fish
12 oz (350 g) smoked cod or haddock
1½ pints (900 ml) milk
4 oz (100 g) butter
4 oz (100 g) flour
1½ level teaspoons salt
½ level teaspoon white pepper
4 oz (100 g) button mushrooms, sliced
2 tablespoons chopped fresh parsley
4 oz (100 g) peeled prawns
2 lb (900 g) potatoes, peeled
a little milk and extra butter for mashing potatoes

Preparation that can be done in advance
The pie can be made up to a day ahead and kept in the refrigerator until required.

Wash both white and smoked fish, put in a saucepan with the milk and simmer gently for 10 minutes, or until the fish can be flaked with a fork. Strain and reserve the milk from the fish, then skin and flake the fish, removing any bones.

Rinse out the saucepan, then melt the butter in it, stir in the flour and cook for 2 minutes, still stirring. Add the milk and bring to the boil, stirring until thickened. Add the salt, pepper, mushrooms, parsley and prawns and simmer for 3 to 4 minutes. Stir in the flaked fish; taste and check the seasoning.

Turn into a shallow 4-pint (2.3 litre) ovenproof dish to cool.

Boil the potatoes, drain and then mash with a little milk, butter and seasoning. Spread over the fish and rough up with a knife or fork.

Reheat when required in a hot oven at 400F (200C) gas 6, for about 45 to 60 minutes until the top is golden brown and the fish mixture heated through and bubbling.

Serves 8

Salmon or Pink Trout en Croûte

A special dish and a real change from the Sunday roast. Make this with a small whole salmon or, more reasonably, use a pink trout from a trout farm. One of about 2½ to 3 lb (1.1 to 1.3 kg) in size is perfect for six people. It is not difficult to bone, providing you have a sharp knife.

2½ lb (1.1 kg) fresh salmon or pink trout, gutted
juice of half a lemon
salt
freshly ground black pepper
4 oz (100 g) butter, softened
½ bunch fresh dill or chives, chopped
14-oz (397-g) packet of puff pastry, thawed
a little beaten egg, to glaze

First bone the fish or ask your fishmonger to do this for you. To do it yourself, take off the head, then fillet the fish by slipping the knife on top of the backbone, then take off the first fillet. Turn over the fish and remove the second fillet in the same way. Remove the skin by placing the fillets skin side down on a board. With a sharp knife and a sawing action, work the knife along the fillet from the tail end, pressing the knife down on to the skin at a diagonal angle until the skin is removed. Pull out any small bones that you see in the flesh.

Squeeze the lemon juice over the fillets and season well. Spread half the butter over one fillet, then sprinkle with chopped dill or chives. Cover with the other fillet of fish and spread with the remaining butter.

Roll out the pastry thinly – you won't need quite all of it. Use to wrap the fish, sealing the pastry well. Brush with beaten egg and keep the folds of the pastry on top, rather than having thick folds underneath. Place on a baking try and chill until ready to bake.

Bake at 425F (220C) gas 7, for about 30 minutes until the pastry is golden brown. Serve at once with Fresh herb cream sauce (page 126) or Hollandaise sauce (page 83).

Serves 6

FRESH HERB CREAM SAUCE

Fresh dill is, I think, preferable to chives for this sauce, but if you haven't any in the garden or can't buy it, chives are nearly as good.

3 oz (75 g) butter, melted
juice of one lemon
1 rounded teaspoon flour
½ pint (300 ml) single cream
1 egg yolk
½ bunch fresh chives or dill, chopped
salt
freshly ground black pepper

Put all the ingredients except the dill or chives in the blender or food processor, or whisk together until smooth. Transfer to a bowl and place over a pan of gently simmering water, and stir until thickened. This will take about 10 minutes.

Taste and check the seasoning; add the dill or chives and serve.

One-Pot Dishes & Casseroles

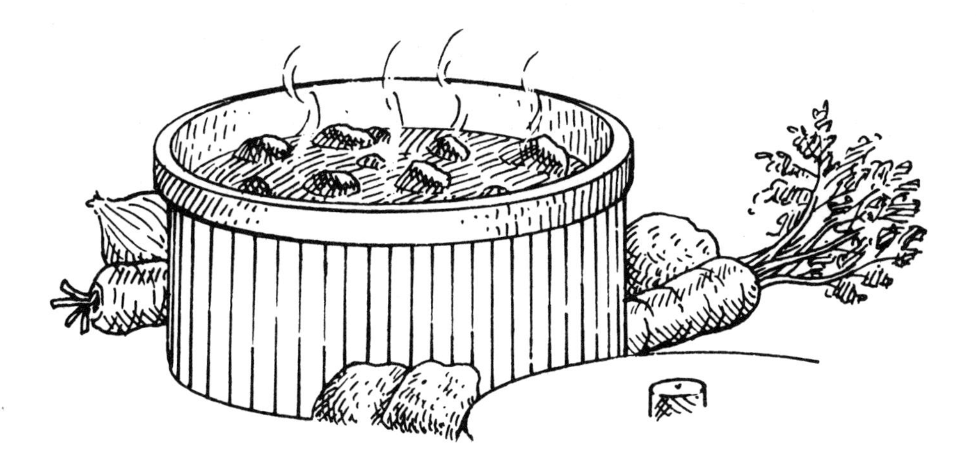

A hearty casserole or stew may not be the first thing that springs to mind when the subject of Sunday lunches is mentioned, but for a change, a one-pot dish has many advantages. It can be prepared the day before, leaving Sunday morning free for other family activities; many stews mellow if left overnight, and they all help the budget by making use of the less tender cuts of meat. The long, slow cooking is done in the oven or on top of the stove at a low temperature and uses less fuel than you would need for the Sunday roast. A casserole can be stretched with added vegetables to cater for unexpected guests, and it will cook away happily if left to itself and the family turn up to eat in relays – as often happens.

If you don't want to serve potatoes – or if potatoes are included in the ingredients as part of the dish – a green vegetable is all you need,

or a layered vegetable 'pie' to cook alongside the casserole. Try a salad of different beans and pulses – aduki beans, haricots, red kidney beans – all cooked then tossed with some crunchy chopped celery in a French dressing made with plenty of lemon juice, and scattered with plenty of fresh chopped herbs or parsley.

Curries, too are popular these days, and a lasagne will be welcomed as an informal change – especially if you have had a weekend of rich food. Add herby dumplings to stretch a casserole still further; use an ovenproof one that's not too large for the amount of meat or you'll lose valuable juices in evaporation; remember when preparing the meat to remove tough gristle but leave a little fat to enrich the sauce. And I'm often asked about stock: I tend to freeze mine in concentrated form, but I'm a fan of stock cubes. I use them a lot – and I wouldn't be without them.

BIG BEEF CASSEROLE

A great favourite in our house. It is important to make it in a very large casserole as the ingredients are added one by one. Add the root vegetables to the meat, then go and have a drink at your local; when you return, stir in the peas and by the time you have laid the table they will be cooked. It is then a complete meal in itself. I usually put it in the centre of the table and let everybody help themselves.

1½ lb (675 g) stewing steak, such as skirt of beef
1½ oz (40 g) dripping
1½ oz (40 g) flour
1 pint beef stock
14 oz (397 g) can peeled tomatoes
about 1½ teaspoons salt
freshly ground black pepper
½ teaspoon mixed dried herbs
1 lb (450 g) mixed root vegetables, such as parsnip, turnip, celery, carrot or swede
1 large onion, chopped
1½ lb (675 g) potatoes, cut in quarters
8 oz (225 g) frozen garden peas

Heat the oven to 325F (160C) gas 3.

Cut the meat into neat cubes about 1 inch (2.5 cm) in diameter.

Melt the dripping in a frying pan and quickly fry the beef to brown it and seal the juices in the meat. Stir in the flour and cook for 2 minutes to brown lightly. Stir in the stock and bring to the boil, stirring until slightly thickened. Turn into a very large casserole about 4- to 5-pint (2.3- to 2.8-litre) in size. Stir in the tomatoes, salt, pepper and dried herbs. Cover the casserole and cook in the oven for 1½ hours.

Add the root vegetables and onion with the potatoes and stir well so that they are well mixed into the casserole and covered by the sauce. Cook for a further 1½ hours.

Remove the casserole from the oven; taste and check the seasoning. Stir in peas and return to the oven for a further 10 minutes.

Serves 6

HOT POT

Cook carrots and celery in the oven alongside this hot pot and you will have a complete, oven-cooked meal.

1 lb (450 g) stewing steak
1½ lb (675 g) potatoes, sliced
2 onions, sliced
14 oz (397 g) can peeled tomatoes
salt and pepper
¼ pint (150 ml) beef stock

Heat the oven to 350F (180C) gas 4.

Cut the meat into neat 1-inch (2.5-cm) cubes.

Place a layer of potato in the bottom of an ovenproof casserole or dish, cover with half the meat, onion and tomatoes and some of the juice from the can and season well. Cover with another layer of potatoes and then add the remaining meat, onion and tomatoes with plenty of seasoning. Finally, arrange the remaining potatoes neatly over the top of the dish. Pour on the stock, cover the dish and cook in the oven for 1½ hours.

Remove the lid and continue cooking for a further ½ hour until the meat and vegetables are tender.

Serves 4

Easy Steak

An ideal meal to leave in the oven to take care of itself on a busySunday morning. Cook jacket potatoes alongside the beef and put a dish of Oven-baked carrots and celery (page 59) on the shelf underneath to make this a complete meal.

1½ pint (82 g) packet tomato soup mix
1½ lb (675 g) chuck steak cut in one piece about 1-inch (2.5-cm) thick
1 oz (25 g) butter
1 onion, chopped
mixed dried herbs to taste
1 tablespoon Worcestershire sauce

Heat the oven to 300F (150C) gas 2.

Take a large piece of foil, lay it on a baking tray and sprinkle with half the soup mix. Lay the beef on top and sprinkle over the remaining soup mix. Dot with butter and cover with the chopped onion. Sprinkle with a few dried herbs and the Worcestershire sauce.

Loosely seal the foil and cook in the oven undisturbed for about 3 hours.

Open the foil and lift the steak on to a warm serving dish. Keep hot.

Scrape the juices from the foil into a saucepan and stir in about ½ pint (300 ml) cold water. Bring to the boil, stirring until thickened, simmer for about 2 minutes. Serve with the beef.

Serves 4

SPICY BEEF CASSOULET

This is an excellent dish for informal entertaining and is delicious if served with a green salad and chunks of French bread.

4 oz (100 g) red kidney beans
½ level teaspoon bicarbonate of soda
1 oz (25 g) flour
1 teaspoon salt
freshly ground black pepper
½ teaspoon ground ginger
1½ lb (675 g) shin of beef cut in 1-inch (2.5-cm) cubes
2 oz (50 g) dripping

Sauce
a few drops of Tabasco sauce
8 oz (225 g) can peeled tomatoes
¼ pint (150 ml) beef stock
2 tablespoons soft brown sugar
4 oz (100 g) mushrooms, sliced
2 tablespoons cider vinegar
2 cloves garlic, crushed
1 bay leaf
1 red pepper

Preparation that can be done ahead

Place the kidney beans in a basin with the bicarbonate of soda, cover with cold water and leave to stand overnight, then drain.

Heat the oven to 325F (160C) gas 3.

Mix the flour, seasoning and ginger together and thoroughly coat the meat.

Melt the dripping in a frying pan and fry the meat quickly to brown on all sides. Lift out with a slotted spoon and place in a casserole with the beans.

Combine all the sauce ingredients, except the red pepper, in a pan and bring to the boil. Pour this over the meat, cover the casserole and cook in the oven for about 2 to 3 hours.

Remove the seeds and white pith from the red pepper and cut into rings. Add to the casserole and return it to the oven to cook for a further 30 minutes or until the beef is tender. Taste and adjust the seasoning and remove the bay leaf before serving.

Serves 4 to 6

Valencia Beef

If you can get pie veal, use this instead of beef for a change. Add the juice of half a lemon, as it helps to bring out the full flavour of the veal.

2 lb (900 g) stewing steak
2 tablespoons corn or vegetable oil
1 oz (25 g) butter
1 large onion, chopped
1 clove garlic, crushed
1½ oz (40 g) flour
¼ pint (150 ml) sweet cider
½ pint (300 ml) beef stock
14-oz (397-g) can chopped tomatoes
1 tablespoon apricot jam
sprig of lemon thyme
good pinch saffron stamens
salt
freshly ground black pepper

Cut the stewing steak into ¾-inch (1.90-cm) pieces. Take a large saucepan, measure in the oil and butter and heat together, then fry the cubes of meat until brown on all sides. Add the onion and garlic with the flour and mix well. Stir in the remaining ingredients, bring to the boil, cover and simmer for about 2 hours. When tender, taste and check the seasoning – and if the sauce is a little thick, thin down with some extra stock.

Turn into a warm serving dish and serve with creamed potatoes and a green vegetable such as broccoli or beans.

Serves 6 to 8

Green Peppercorn Steak

If you like Pepper steak you will like this; it is hot and really not suitable for children. If you have no dried peppercorns, use canned ones and just add them to the sauce.

6 slices silverside of beef, each about 5 oz (150 g) in weight
1 tablespoon dried green peppercorns, crushed
2 tablespoons vegetable oil
1 oz (25 g) butter
2 large onions, sliced
3 cloves garlic, crushed
1½ oz (40 g) flour
½ pint (300 ml) beef stock
½ pint (300 ml) white wine
1 teaspoon salt

Heat the oven to 350F (180C) gas 4.

Coat the slices of silverside with the crushed peppercorns, pushing them firmly on to the meat.

In a large flameproof casserole, heat the oil and fry the steaks, two at a time, for about 2 minutes on each side to seal in the juices. Lift out on to a plate and leave on one side.

Wipe the casserole with a piece of kitchen paper, then melt the butter and fry the onions until golden brown. Add the garlic and stir in the flour. Gradually blend in the stock and wine and bring to the boil, stirring continuously until the sauce has thickened. Remove from the heat and return the steaks to the casserole; sprinkle over the salt. Cover the casserole and cook in the oven for about 1½ hours, or until the steak is tender.

Serves 6

CHILLI CON CARNE

If you like your chilli very hot add more powder; take care, though, as the different brands vary considerably in spiciness.

8 oz (225 g) kidney beans
4 rashers streaky bacon, cut in strips
2 onions, chopped
1½ lb (675 g) minced beef
1 large clove garlic, crushed
1½ oz (40 g) flour
1 to 2 level teaspoons chilli powder
14-oz (397-g) can peeled tomatoes
½ pint beef stock
1½ level teaspoons salt
freshly ground black pepper
1 large green pepper, sliced

Preparation that can be done in advance
Put the kidney beans in a bowl, cover with cold water and leave to soak overnight.

The following day drain the beans, cover with fresh cold water in a saucepan and bring to the boil and simmer for 20 minutes, then drain.

Meanwhile, put the bacon, onions, minced beef and garlic in a saucepan and fry gently for 5 to 10 minutes, stirring frequently, until the meat is lightly browned and the fat has run out. Stir in the flour and chilli powder to taste and cook for a minute. Add the tomatoes and stock and bring to the boil, stirring. Season well, then cover the saucepan and simmer for 45 minutes.

Add the green pepper and continue cooking for a further 15 minutes, or until the beans are tender.

Taste and check the seasoning, then turn into a serving dish and serve with a bowl of plain boiled rice and a crisp green salad.

Serves 6

Bobotie

A South African dish and a very interesting variation on the minced beef theme. It makes a deliciously spicy Sunday lunch dish.

2 lb (1 kg) raw minced beef
2 onions, chopped
1 thick slice white bread, with crusts removed
½ pint (300 ml) milk
1 tablespoon curry powder
1 tablespoon sugar
3 teaspoons salt
plenty of freshly ground black pepper
1 tablespoon turmeric
2 tablespoons lemon juice
1 oz (25 g) sliced almonds
3 oz (75 g) sultanas
3 tablespoons chutney
2 eggs
4 bay leaves

Heat the oven to 350F (180C) gas 4. Grease a 3-pint (1.7-litre) ovenproof dish.

In a large frying pan, spread out the minced beef and cook gently until the fat begins to run out of the meat, then add the onion and increase the heat to brown the meat and onions.

Soak the bread in the milk, then squeeze out the excess liquid and keep on one side. Crumble the bread into the meat and add all the remaining ingredients except the reserved milk, the eggs and bay leaves. Mix thoroughly, then turn this mixture into the dish and bake in the oven for 45 minutes.

Beat the eggs and milk together and pour over the meat. Arrange the bay leaves on top and return to the oven for a further 15 minutes until set.

Serves 6 to 8

SUNDAY COTTAGE PIE

This is an ideal choice for an inexpensive family lunch at the end of a busy week.

1½ lb (675 g) raw minced beef
1 large onion, chopped
2 carrots, diced
¼ teaspoon mixed dried herbs
2 level teaspoons tomato purée
1 oz (25 g) flour
½ pint (300 ml) beef stock
1 level teaspoon salt
freshly ground black pepper
2 lb potatoes
1 oz (25 g) butter
a little milk

Preparation that can be done ahead
The pie may be completely assembled, then kept in the refrigerator until required, and then baked.

Put the mince in a saucepan and cook over a moderate heat to let the fat run out; add the onion and carrot and fry until the meat is brown, about 10 minutes. Stir in the herbs, tomato purée and flour and cook for a minute. Add the stock and seasoning and bring to the boil, stirring until the mixture has thickened. Cover the saucepan and simmer for about 45 minutes, or until the meat and vegetables are tender. Turn into a 2½-pint (1.4-litre) ovenproof dish and leave to cool.

Heat the oven to 375F (190C) gas 5.

Cook the potatoes in boiling salted water until tender. Drain well and mash with butter and milk and season to taste. Spread over the top of the pie. Bake in the oven for about 40 to 45 minutes until the pie is hot through and the potato is tinged golden brown.

Serves 4 to 6

Oxford Meatballs

Serve with plain boiled rice and a side salad; ideal for a crowd.

Meatballs
1½ lb (675 g) raw minced beef
4 oz (100 g) fresh white breadcrumbs
2 eggs
2 teaspoons salt
freshly ground black pepper
4 tablespoons oil

Sauce
12 oz (350 g) onions, sliced
2 cloves garlic, crushed
3 oz (75 g) flour
8 oz (225 g) mushrooms, sliced
1 large green pepper, seeded and sliced
½ pint (300 ml) beef stock

Preparation that can be done ahead
The dish may be made ahead and reheated when required.

First make the meatballs. Place the minced beef, breadcrumbs, eggs and seasoning in a bowl and mix well. Turn on to a floured surface and shape into about 30 meatballs. Heat the oil in a large pan and fry the meatballs for about 15 minutes or until brown all over. Lift them out with a slotted spoon and put on one side to drain on kitchen paper.

For the sauce, add the onions and garlic to the fat remaining in the pan and fry for about 5 minutes, stirring, until golden brown. Stir in the flour, then add the remaining ingredients and bring to the boil, stirring until the sauce has thickened. Return the meatballs to the pan, cover with a lid or piece of foil and cook gently for about 30 minutes, until the meatballs are tender. Taste and check the seasoning, then turn into a warm serving dish.

Serves 8

Beef Provençale

A good-natured casserole that will wait happily in the oven for an hour on a very low heat.

1½ lb (675 g) stewing steak
3 tablespoons oil
2 large onions, finely sliced
1 clove garlic, crushed
1½ oz (40 g) flour
14-oz (397-g) can peeled tomatoes
¼ pint (150 ml) beef stock
salt and pepper
1 green pepper, sliced
½ teaspoon mixed dried herbs

Heat the oven to 325F (160C) gas 3.

Cut the meat into strips about 2 inches (5 cm) long and ½ inch (1.25 cm) wide.

Heat the oil in a large pan and quickly fry the meat with the onion and garlic until the meat is brown, then lift out with a slotted spoon and put in a casserole. Stir the flour into the fat remaining in the pan and cook for a minute. Add all the remaining ingredients to the pan and bring to the boil, stirring. Pour into the casserole, stir into the meat and onions, then cover with a tight-fitting lid and cook in the oven for about 2 hours, or until tender. Taste and check seasoning before serving.

In winter this is nice with jacket potatoes cooked alongside the casserole, but I like it best served with buttered noodles and plenty of freshly ground black pepper.

Serves 4

HEARTY BEEF CASSEROLE

This is a cheat! But it is ideal when you have an action-packed weekend with the family.

a 1-pint (600-ml) packet 'Hearty' vegetable and beef soup
about ¾ pint (450 ml) water
1 lb (450 g) stewing steak

Heat the oven to 325F (160C) gas 3.

Sprinkle the soup into a casserole or ovenproof dish and stir in the water to blend well.

Cut the steak into neat 1-inch (2.5-cm) cubes and stir into the casserole; cover with a tight-fitting lid and cook in the oven for about 2½ to 3 hours, or until the meat is tender. It is a good idea to take the casserole from the oven after the first hour and give it a stir, but if you are out do not worry!

Taste and check seasoning before serving; if you find the casserole is too thick add a spoonful or two of hot water.

This is another good dish if served with jacket potatoes cooked alongside the casserole and Oven-baked carrots and celery (page 59).

Serves 4

OISEAUX SANS TÊTES

These little beef parcels certainly take time to make, but you will be delighted with the result. They have a crunchy chestnut filling in a rich onion sauce. Dried chestnuts are sometimes difficult to obtain except at Christmastime, but try health food shops or a good delicatessen. Well worth remembering, too, that they are cheap to buy in Spain and other European countries, where they grow in abundance, and are sold from sacks in the town markets – should you be on holiday.

If dried chestnuts are not available, use a 15 oz (425 g) can of whole chestnuts in water. Drain and coarsely chop them.

8 thin slices of silverside of beef, weighing about 3 to 4 oz (75 to 100 g) each
8 wooden cocktail sticks

Stuffing
4 oz (100 g) dried chestnuts
3 oz (75 g) streaky bacon, chopped
small onion, finely chopped
6 oz (175 g) pork sausagemeat
salt and freshly ground black pepper

Sauce
5 tablespoons oil
1 large onion, chopped
2 oz (50 g) flour
½ pint (300 ml) red wine
½ pint (300 ml) beef stock
2 teaspoons tomato purée

Cover the chestnuts with warm water and leave to soak overnight.

Preparation that can be done ahead
Prepare as far as ready for the oven; cover, put in the refrigerator and cook when required.

Next day, drain the chestnuts, cover with cold water, bring to the boil and simmer until just tender, about 45 minutes, then drain and cool. Peel off any bits of brown skin and chop fairly coarsely. Put the bacon into a non-stick frying pan and allow fat to run out for a few minutes, then add onion and brown both over a moderate heat. Stir in the chestnuts, then cool and mix with the sausagemeat and a little salt and pepper. If time allows, chill this mixture so it will firm up.

Beat out the meat to make it thinner and easier to roll up: split open a polythene bag to make two pieces. Sandwich a piece of meat between the pieces of polythene and beat out the meat with a rolling pin. Repeat with the other slices of meat. Place the pieces of meat flat on a board and divide the stuffing between them; roll up and secure each one with a wooden cocktail stick.

Heat the oven 350F (180C) gas 4.

Heat the 5 tablespoons oil in a pan and fry the meat rolls on all sides over a brisk heat until brown, remove the cocktail sticks and transfer the rolls to an ovenproof casserole. Add the onion to the pan and cook for about 5 minutes, stirring, until golden brown. Stir in the flour and cook for a minute. Blend in the wine and bring to the boil, stirring, then thin down with the stock until you have a good, thick sauce. Add the purée and seasoning to taste. Pour over the beef rolls. Cover and cook in the oven for about an hour, or until the meat is tender. Taste, check the seasoning and serve piping hot.

Serves 8

Pork Chops Ratatouille

The vegetables make a lovely combination with pork and all that is really needed is chunks of crusty French bread to serve with it.

3 tablespoons oil
2 green peppers, sliced
2 onions, sliced
1 clove garlic, crushed
4 pork chops or steaks
a little butter
12 oz (350 g) courgettes, sliced
12 oz (350 g) tomatoes, peeled and quartered
salt and freshly ground black pepper

Heat the oil in a large pan, add the peppers, onion and garlic, then cover the pan and cook over a low-to-moderate heat for 10 minutes, until the vegetables are soft but not brown.

Meanwhile in another pan, fry the pork chops quickly in the butter to brown them on both sides.

Stir the courgettes and tomatoes into the other vegetables and season well. Lay the chops on top, cover the pan and cook for 10 minutes, then remove the lid, turn the chops over and continue cooking over a moderate heat for a further 10 minutes, or until the meat is tender.

Taste and check the seasoning, then arrange the chops on a warm serving dish and spoon the vegetables around.

Serves 4

PORK GOULASH

Buy pie pork for this recipe; it is reasonable in price and with slow-cooking is full of flavour and very tender. This recipe is good to serve with plain boiled noodles.

1½ lb (675 g) boneless lean pork, such as shoulder
2 tablespoons oil
2 onions, sliced
1 green pepper, seeded and diced
14-oz (397-g) can peeled tomatoes
¼ pint stock
1½ level teaspoons salt
freshly ground black pepper
3 level teaspoons paprika
2 level tablespoons cornflour
2 tablespoons cold water

Trim any excess fat from the pork and cut into 1-inch (2.5-cm) cubes. Heat the oil in a saucepan, add the meat, onion and pepper and fry for 5 minutes. Add the contents of the can of tomatoes, stock, salt, pepper and paprika and bring to the boil, stirring constantly.

Reduce the heat and then cover the saucepan and simmer very gently for 1½ to 2 hours, or until the pork is tender.

Blend the cornflour to a smooth paste with the water and add to the pan, stirring well until the sauce has thickened slightly. Taste and check seasoning and then turn into a warm serving dish.

Serves 4 to 6

Pork and Prune Stew with Parsley Dumplings

This recipe was given to me by Anne Dare of British Meat, who rightly says it tastes as good as it looks. The dumplings help to stretch the meat and the prunes add a good flavour.

2 tablespoons oil
4 medium onions, sliced
1 lb (450 g) lean bladebone pork, cubed
1 lb (450 g) carrots, sliced
2 tablespoons flour
1 pint (600 ml) stock
1 bay leaf
salt and freshly ground black pepper
4 oz (100 g) stoned prunes, soaked overnight in cold water

Dumplings
4 oz (100 g) self-raising flour
2 oz (50 g) suet, shredded
2 tablespoons chopped parsley
grated rind and juice of one lemon
salt and pepper

Heat the oil in a large flameproof casserole and brown the onions, lift them from the pan with a slotted spoon, add the pork to the pan and fry until nicely browned. Replace the onions, add the carrots and heat through, stirring, for a few minutes. Blend in flour, add the stock, bay leaf, seasoning and drained prunes. Cover and simmer gently for 2 hours, until the meat is tender.

To make the dumplings: mix all the ingredients to a soft dough with a little water. Divide the mixture into 8 small dumplings and place on top of the casserole 20 minutes before the end of the cooking time. Cover and simmer until the dumplings are light and well risen before serving.

Serves 6

AMERICAN-STYLE SPARE RIBS

I like these served with oven-baked jacket potatoes or warm bread rolls. The ribs are succulent, but messy, so it is best to have an ample supply of paper napkins on hand.

2 tablespoons oil
12 oz (350 g) onions, chopped
2 cloves garlic, crushed
2 tablespoons vinegar
2 tablespoons Worcestershire sauce
2½ oz (62 g) can tomato purée
¼ teaspoon chilli powder
6 tablespoons clear honey
½ pint (300 ml) water
2½ lb (1.1 kg) pork ribs
salt and freshly ground black pepper

Heat the oven to 350F (180C) gas 4.

Heat the oil in a large saucepan, add the onions and fry gently for 15 minutes, or until they are pale golden brown and soft. Add all the remaining ingredients except the ribs, salt and pepper and bring to the boil, stirring constantly. Simmer uncovered for about 10 minutes.

Arrange the ribs in a single layer in a shallow ovenproof dish, season with salt and pepper and pour over half the sauce. Cook in the oven for about an hour, then remove and drain off any surplus fat or oil and blot with kitchen paper.

Coat the ribs with the remaining sauce, return them to the oven and cook for a further 20 to 30 minutes, or until golden brown and the ribs are very tender.

Serves 4

PORK AND PINEAPPLE CURRY

This is a slightly sweet, spiced curry that always goes down well.

2 lb (900 g) lean pork
1½ oz (40 g) flour
1½ teaspoons salt
1 large onion, chopped
2 oz (50 g) margarine
1 level tablespoon hot curry powder, or to taste
1 level tablespoon paprika
½ pint (300 ml) stock
2 dried red chillies
1 tablespoon mango chutney
1 lb (450 g) can pineapple cubes
2 bay leaves

Cut the pork into 1-inch (2.5-cm) cubes and toss in the flour and salt. Put the onion and margarine in a saucepan and fry for 5 minutes; stir in the curry powder and paprika and cook for a further 5 minutes over a gentle heat, then add the pork and stir well. Fry for another 5 minutes. Add all the remaining ingredients to the pan including the pineapple syrup, cover and cook very gently for 1½ to 2 hours, or until the pork is tender. If preferred, the curry can be put into a casserole and cooked in the oven at 160C (325F) gas 3, for about the same time.

All curries should be cooked long and slow to bring out the best flavour. Remove all the bay leaves and chillies, taste and check the seasoning and serve with boiled rice and the following side dishes.

Serves 6 to 8

ACCOMPANIMENTS FOR CURRY

Rice
Use basmati or long-grain rice and allow about 2 oz (50 g) of uncooked rice per person. Cook in plenty of salted water until just tender. Drain well.

Poppodums fried in deep fat and served in a stack are also put on the table.

SIDE DISHES also called Sambols

Cucumber, yogurt and mint
Mix 1 tablespoon chopped mint with 3 inches (7.5 cm) diced cucumber and ¼ pint (150 ml) natural yogurt. Season well.

Banana
2 bananas, sliced and tossed in lemon juice.

Onion and green pepper
1 mild onion, finely chopped or sliced, mixed with a finely chopped or sliced green pepper.

Mango chutney
This is best bought ready-made.

Egg
Slices of hard-boiled egg

Nuts
A bowl of mixed salted nuts

Tomatoes
A bowl of tomato slices

Coconut
A bowl of plain desiccated coconut served just as it is, goes very well with a spicy curry.

RATASKA

A tasty combination of ratatouille and moussaka with less aubergine but lots of other colourful Mediterranean vegetables. A perfect way of using up some of the midsummer glut of courgettes. It is very important to make this in a shallow dish so that everyone gets some of the brown cheese topping.

1½ lb (675 g) raw minced shoulder lamb (from a small shoulder)
1 lb (450 g) onions, chopped
2 fat cloves garlic, crushed
1 red pepper, seeded and roughly chopped
1½ oz (40 g) flour
¼ pint (150 ml) stock
14 oz (400 g) can peeled tomatoes
a good teaspoon salt and plenty of freshly ground black pepper
a level teaspoon dried rosemary
1 lb (450 g) small courgettes, sliced
1 aubergine, thinly sliced

Sauce
1½ oz (40 g) butter
1½ oz (40 g) flour
¾ pint (450 ml) milk
1 level teaspoon Dijon mustard
a pinch grated nutmeg
salt and pepper
4 oz (100 g) Gouda cheese, grated
1 egg, beaten

Preparation that can be done ahead
The dish is really best cooked freshly, but it may be cooked through and kept in the refrigerator overnight, and reheated when required.

Heat the oven to 375F (190C) gas 5. Grease a large, shallow ovenproof dish about 3 pint (1.7 litre).

Spread out the minced lamb in a large frying pan and fry over a low heat until the fat runs out, stirring to prevent sticking. Add the onion, garlic and red pepper and increase the heat to brown the meat and vegetables. Stir in the flour and cook for a few minutes, then add the stock and tomatoes with their juice, and stir until the mixture has thickened. Season well and add the rosemary and courgettes. Turn into the greased dish.

Rinse out the pan and fill to a third full with water; bring to the boil, add the sliced aubergine and cook it for a minute, then drain well. This makes the aubergine tender and prevents it discolouring. Arrange the slices on top of the meat.

Now make the sauce: melt the butter in a saucepan, add the flour and cook for a few minutes without it colouring. Blend in the milk and bring to the boil, stirring until thickened. Add the mustard, nutmeg, seasoning and cheese and mix well. Draw the pan from the heat and beat in the egg. Pour the sauce over the aubergines.

Cook, uncovered, for about an hour in the oven, until the top is a pale golden brown.

Serve with hot rolls or herb bread.

Note: You can also use the same amount of minced beef instead of lamb, but the result is not quite so good.

Serves 6

CASSOULET

A traditional French dish that should be made using goose or mutton. In England it is not so easy to obtain these meats, so I have used lean lamb. This is a dish that is a meal in itself, very good-natured and one that sits happily in the oven on a lower heat waiting to be served.

12 oz (350 g) haricot beans
1½ pints (900 ml) water
6 oz (175 g) streaky unsmoked bacon or salt belly of pork
1 neck fillet of lamb or about 12 oz (350 g) lean lamb
2 onions, sliced
3–cloves garlic, crushed
8 oz (225 g) tomatoes, peeled and quartered
1 tablespoon tomato purée
2 garlic sausages, sliced
salt and freshly ground black pepper
3 to 4 oz (75 to 100 g) fresh breadcrumbs

Wash the beans, cover with water and leave to soak overnight, or for at least 12 hours. Next day, drain the beans and discard the soaking water; place in a saucepan with the 1½ pints (900 ml) water and bring to the boil, then lower the heat and simmer for 30 minutes. Do not add salt at this stage as it toughens the beans.

Heat the oven to 275F (140C) gas 1.

Remove the rind and any bone from the bacon or pork and cut into neat strips. Cut the lamb in slices and put both in a large casserole- about 4½ pints (2.5 litres). Add the onions, garlic, tomatoes, purée, garlic sausage and seasoning. When the beans have simmered for 30 minutes, pour them into the casserole with their water, stir well, then cover and cook in the oven for 3 hours.

Remove the lid and sprinkle the top with the breadcrumbs; return to the oven for a further 30 minutes. The breadcrumbs do not brown, but just form a crust across the top of the dish.

Serves 6

COUNTRYMAN'S KIDNEYS

These kidneys in a rich sauce make a delicious meal if served with plain boiled noodles, and a green vegetable such as broccoli.

12 pickling onions
8 pork chipolata sausages
8 lambs kidneys
1 oz (25 g) butter
1 oz (25 g) flour
¼ pint (150 ml) red wine
¼ pint (150 ml) stock
1 tablespoon tomato purée
salt and pepper

Peel the pickling onions carefully, just trimming off the minimum at the top and base so that they will stay whole. Place in a saucepan, cover with cold water and bring to the boil, then simmer for 5 minutes and drain well.

Twist each sausage in half and cut. Peel the thin skin off the kidneys and then cut in half horizontally. Remove the cores and slice the kidneys.

Melt the butter in a saucepan, add the kidneys and sausages and fry quickly to brown. Lift out with a slotted spoon and put on a warm plate.

Stir the flour into the fat remaining in the pan and cook for a minute. Add the wine and stock and bring to the boil, stirring. Blend in the tomato purée and seasoning, then return the sausages and kidneys to the pan with the pickling onions. Cover and simmer gently for 20 minutes.

Taste, adjust seasoning and turn into a warm serving dish.

Serves 4

VEAL FRICASSÉE

A light stew, served in a cream and mushroom sauce, that makes a pleasant change from the usual beef casseroles.

1½ lb (675 g) pie veal
2 onions, sliced
2 carrots, sliced
1 bay leaf
juice of half a lemon
salt and pepper
6 oz (175 g) button mushrooms, quartered
2 oz (50 g) butter
2 oz (50 g) flour
3 to 4 tablespoons double cream
freshly chopped fresh parsley

Cut the veal into neat 1-inch (2.5-cm) cubes. Place in a saucepan, cover with cold water and then bring to the boil; lift off the scum with a slotted spoon and then drain the veal. Place the veal back in the saucepan with the onions, carrots and bay leaf and cover with 1½ pints (900 ml) water; add the lemon juice and salt and pepper. Bring to the boil and simmer for an hour, then add the mushrooms and cook for a further 30 to 45 minutes or until the veal is tender.

Lift out the veal and vegetables with a slotted spoon and put in a dish. Remove the bay leaf. Pour off a pint of veal stock and keep the remainder to use in another recipe, or for soup.

Melt the butter in the saucepan, stir in the flour and cook for a minute. Remove the pan from the heat and blend in the warm stock, then return to the heat and cook until thickened – about 2 minutes. Return the meat and vegetables to the sauce and bring to the boil, stirring. Taste and check the seasoning.

When ready to serve, stir in the cream and heat through. Turn into a hot dish and sprinkle with parsley.

Serves 6

Normandy Pheasant

The cooking time for the pheasant will depend on its age; an old bird will take up to 2½ hours. A plump pheasant will serve four people if divided into four joints, or if preferred, the meat can be carved off the carcass.

1 good-sized roasting pheasant
1 tablespoon corn or salad oil
2 oz (50 g) bacon (2 to 3 rashers), finely chopped
1 large onion, chopped
1 clove garlic, crushed
4 small cooking apples, peeled, cored and sliced
1 oz (25 g) flour
½ pint (300 ml) sweet cider
salt
freshly ground black pepper
chopped parsley

Heat the oven to 350F (180C) gas 4. Wipe the pheasant with damp paper. Heat the oil in a large frying pan and fry the pheasant until lightly browned all over; lift out and put in a large ovenproof casserole.

Add the bacon, onion and garlic to the fat remaining in the pan and fry for about 10 minutes until brown, then spoon over the pheasant with a slotted spoon to leave the fat in the pan. Add the apple slices to the casserole. Stir the flour into the fat remaining in the pan and then gradually add the cider and bring to the boil, stirring until thickened. Season to taste and then pour over the pheasant. Cover and cook in the oven for about an hour, or until the pheasant is tender; when the thigh is pricked with a skewer the juices should run clear.

Lift the pheasant out of the dish and carve into four portions – two legs and two breasts. Spoon the apple mixture into a processor or blender and reduce to a purée. Put in a saucepan and bring to the boil, diluting with a little stock if too thick and taste and check the seasoning. Serve with the pheasant, and scatter dish with parsley.

Serves 4

DEVILLED CHICKEN

This is one of those recipes that can quite easily be increased to feed any number of people. Serve with a bowl of spicy rice and a crisp green salad.

salt and freshly ground black pepper
4 roasting chicken thigh joints

Sauce
1 rounded tablespoon apricot jam
1 teaspoon Dijon mustard
pinch cayenne pepper
1 clove garlic, crushed
1 tablespoon Worcestershire sauce
3 tablespoons tomato ketchup
1 tablespoon soy sauce

Heat the oven to 350F (180C) gas 4.

Season the chicken joints well on all sides and put in a shallow ovenproof dish, so that they just touch.

Place all the sauce ingredients in a bowl and blend together, add a little salt and pepper and then pour over the chicken, coating evenly.

Bake in the oven for about an hour; this is best cooked towards the top of the oven. To test when the chicken is cooked, prod the thickest part of the thigh with a skewer. If the juices run clear the chicken is cooked; if still pink, return the chicken to the oven and cook a little longer.

Serve straight from the dish in which it is cooked.

Serves 4

CHICKEN CURRY FOR A CROWD

This Indian curry is authentic and uses no flour to thicken; if you like it stronger, add more curry powder

5 tablespoons corn or vegetable oil
1½ lb (675 g) onions, chopped
4 tablespoons curry powder
14 oz (397 g) can peeled tomatoes
4 generous tablespoons tomato purée
12 chicken thighs, skinned
1 pint (600 ml) water
3 fat cloves garlic
2 teaspoons salt
a piece of fresh ginger, the size of a large walnut, peeled and finely chopped

Take a large heavy saucepan and measure in the oil; add the onions and fry until they are an even golden colour, taking care not to let them catch and brown as this will spoil the flavour. Add the curry powder, tomatoes and purée and cook over a medium heat, without a lid, stirring until the oil starts to come through slightly. Add the chicken, cover with a lid and simmer for 15 minutes. Remove the lid, add the water, garlic, salt and ginger, then cover the pan again and simmer for about 30 minutes, or until the chicken is tender.

Taste and check the seasoning, then serve in a large dish with a big bowl of rice and side dishes (see page 149).

Serves 12

Chicken in Sherry Sauce

Chicken and sherry make a lovely combination. This is a simple meal to prepare – just cook the chicken and make the sauce; when ready to serve, reheat and as soon as the dish is thoroughly hot, remove the pan from the heat and stir in the cream just before serving. It makes a quickly prepared Sunday lunch.

4 chicken portions
2 oz (50 g) butter

Sauce
1½ oz (40 g) flour
½ pint (300 ml) chicken stock
4 oz (100 g) mushrooms, quartered
3 tablespoons sherry
salt
plenty of freshly ground black pepper
¼ pint (300 ml) single cream

Trim any excess lumps of fat from the chicken and any pieces of bone.

Melt the butter in a frying pan, add the chicken portions and cook gently over a moderate heat for 20 to 25 minutes, turning once until the chicken is golden brown on both sides. Pierce the chicken at the thickest point and if the juices run clear, it is cooked. If the juices are still slightly pink, cook the chicken for a little longer.

Lift out and place on a warm serving dish.

Stir the flour into the butter remaining in the pan and cook for a minute. Blend in the stock and bring to the boil, stirring until thickened. Add the mushrooms, sherry and seasoning, and cook gently for 3 to 4 minutes. Taste the sauce, adjust the seasoning, then remove the pan from the heat. Stir in the cream, pour the sauce over the chicken and serve at once.

Serves 4

CHICKEN WITH LEMON

Delicious served with new carrots tossed in butter and chopped parsley.

2 oz (50 g) butter
4 chicken joints, skinned
1 small onion, chopped
1 oz (25 g) flour
grated rind and juice of 2 lemons
½ pint (300 ml) chicken stock
3 to 4 tablespoons double cream
1 tablespoon chopped chives
1 teaspoon salt
freshly ground black pepper

Melt the butter in a large saucepan, add the chicken joints and cook gently for about 5 minutes until golden brown. Lift out of the pan with a slotted spoon and place on a plate.

Add the onion to the pan and cook for about 2 minutes until soft; stir in the flour and cook for a minute. Gradually add the lemon rind and juice, and stock, stirring continuously until thickened. Replace the chicken in the sauce, cover the pan and cook gently for 25 to 30 minutes or until the chicken is tender.

Lift the chicken joints out of the pan and arrange in a warm serving dish. Stir in the double cream, chives and seasoning to taste. Heat the sauce until bubbles just start to break on the surface, then pour over the chicken and serve at once.

Serves 4

Cheese and Pineapple Chicken

Cheese and pineapple make an unusual and tasty combination with chicken.

4 chicken joints, skinned
a little seasoned flour
2 oz (50 g) butter
1 small onion, sliced
½ pint (300 ml) chicken stock
1 tablespoon chopped fresh mixed herbs
salt and freshly ground black pepper
1 level tablespoon cornflour
15 oz (425 g) can pineapple pieces
6 oz (175 g) Cheddar cheese, grated

Coat the chicken in seasoned flour. Melt the butter in a large pan and fry the chicken joints for about 5 minutes until the outsides are golden brown. Lift out with a slotted spoon and put on a plate.

Add the onion to the pan and fry for 5 minutes until golden brown, then return the chicken to the pan, add the stock, mixed herbs and plenty of seasoning. Cover the pan with a lid and simmer gently for about 30 minutes until the chicken is tender. Lift out of the pan, using a slotted spoon, and arrange on an ovenproof serving dish and keep warm.

Blend the cornflour with the juice from the pineapple and stir into the stock in the saucepan. Bring to the boil, stirring continuously until the sauce has thickened, then simmer for 2 minutes.

Remove the pan from the heat and add about two-thirds of the cheese to the sauce. Arrange the pineapple pieces over the chicken, then taste the sauce, check the seasoning and pour over the chicken. Sprinkle with the rest of the cheese and put the dish under a pre-heated hot grill for about 5 minutes, or until the cheese is golden brown and bubbling.

Serves 4

Chicken à la Crème

This is a quick Sunday casserole that doesn't need pre-frying and can be put in the oven to look after itself.

3½ lb (1.5 kg) chicken, skinned and quartered
10.4 oz (295 g) can condensed mushroom soup
¼ pint (150 ml) sweet cider
2 tablespoons Worcestershire sauce
1 teaspoon salt
1 large onion, chopped
8 oz (225 g) button mushrooms, sliced
a little paprika

Heat the oven to 350F (180C) gas 4.

Arrange the chicken joints in the base of a shallow 2½-pint (1.4 litre) ovenproof dish.

In a bowl, mix the remainder of the ingredients until well blended, then pour over the chicken joints. Sprinkle with a little paprika.

Bake, uncovered, for about an hour, or until the chicken is tender; pierce the thickest part of the leg with a skewer to see if the juices run clear. Taste the sauce and check the seasoning. Serve straight from the dish in which it has been cooked, with plain boiled rice and green peas.

Serves 4

Debbie's Chicken

A quick, simple and colourful casserole: no thickening is needed, as the sauce makes itself from the vegetable mixture. If you have fresh basil in the garden, use this instead of rosemary.

1 oz (25 g) butter
1 tablespoon oil
4 chicken thighs
14 oz (397 g) can peeled tomatoes
2 teaspoons sugar
about 6 sticks celery, chopped
1 large onion, chopped
1 teaspoon salt
freshly ground black pepper
1 teaspoon dried rosemary

Heat the oven to 350F (180C) gas 4.

Measure the butter and oil into a frying pan and heat together, then fry the chicken pieces until golden brown on all sides.

Place the remaining ingredients in a shallow ovenproof dish and mix together. Lay the chicken thighs on top and bake, uncovered, for about 1¼ hours, or until the vegetables are tender and the juices from the chicken run clear. Serve straight from the dish in which it is cooked.

Serves 4

GARDENER'S CHICKEN

A very tasty way of serving chicken thighs, and another recipe that can be adapted to serve any number of people.

1½ lb (675 g) parsnips
butter
salt
freshly ground black pepper
4 chicken thigh joints
4 rashers back bacon, with the rind removed

Heat the oven to 375F (190C) gas 5.

Peel the parsnips, cut in quarters and remove the hard core from the centre, then cut the parsnips into neat strips. Place in a saucepan, cover with cold water, bring to the boil and cook for a minute. Drain thoroughly and place in a shallow ovenproof dish, dot with butter and season well with salt and plenty of freshly ground black pepper.

Trim any excess fat from the chicken thighs, then wrap each in a rasher of bacon and place on top of the parsnips.

Bake in the oven for about 35 to 40 minutes when the parsnips will be tender and the juices from the chicken will run clear if pricked with a skewer. Serve straight from the dish with butter spooned over the chicken.

Serves 4

Gougère

An ideal light lunch for a weekend of rather rich food.

Choux pastry
½ pint (300 ml) water
4 oz (100 g) butter
5 oz (150 g) plain flour
4 eggs, beaten
2 oz (50 g) Cheddar cheese, coarsely grated
½ teaspoon salt

Filling
1½ oz (40 g) butter
1 onion, chopped
2 level teaspoons paprika
1 oz (25 g) plain flour
½ pint (300 ml) chicken stock
8 oz (225 g) cooked, diced chicken
8 oz (225 g) cooked, diced ham
salt and pepper

Make the pastry: place the water and butter in a saucepan and bring slowly to the boil. Allow the butter to melt. Remove from the heat and stir in the flour all at once, and beat vigorously until thick and smooth and the mixture leaves the sides of the pan clean. Cool slightly, then beat in the eggs a little at a time until all have been added and the mixture is smooth and glossy. Beat in the cheese and salt.

For the filling: melt the butter and fry the onion for about 5 minutes until soft but not brown. Stir in the paprika and flour and cook for a minute. Add the stock and bring to the boil, stirring until thickened. Add the chicken and ham and heat through, then add seasoning.

Heat the oven to 400F (100C) gas 6, and grease the base and sides of a 3-pint (1.7-litre) shallow ovenproof dish. Spoon the choux paste around the edge of the dish to form an even border and then place the filling in the centre. Bake for 35 to 45 minutes, or until the paste is well risen and golden brown.

Serves 6 to 8

Ham and Egg Pie

Bacon hocks are inexpensive and it is surprising how much meat you can get off them, usually about 1¼ lb (550 g) per hock. As a variation, use 8 oz (225 g) broad beans in place of the eggs.

4 hard-boiled eggs
8 oz (25 g) cooked boiled bacon from a hock
1½ oz (40 g) butter
1½ oz (40 g) flour
¾ pint (450 ml) milk and bacon stock mixed
salt and pepper
2 tablespoons chopped parsley
8 oz (227 g) packet frozen puff pastry, thawed
a little beaten egg or milk to glaze

Preparation that can be done ahead
The pie may be made, covered with pastry, then kept in the refrigerator for a few hours before baking.

Heat the oven to 425F (220C) gas 7.

Quarter the eggs and put them in a 2½-pint (1.4-litre) pie dish. Cut the bacon into a neat ½-inch (1.25-cm) cubes and put on one side.

Melt the butter in a saucepan, stir in the flour and cook for a minute, add the milk mixture and bring to the boil, stirring until the sauce has thickened. Season well and then stir in the parsley and bacon and mix thoroughly. Pour into the pie dish on top of the eggs.

Roll out the pastry to fit the pie dish, cover the pie and seal the edges firmly, using any trimmings to decorate the top with pastry leaves. Make a small slit in the centre for the steam to escape. Glaze the pie with a little beaten egg or milk and bake in the oven for about 30 minutes, when the pie will be thoroughly hot and the pastry well risen and golden brown.

Serve with a green vegetable and, if liked, cook whole tomatoes in the oven underneath the pie.

Serves 6

LASAGNE

Lasagne makes a highly popular and practical dish for an informal lunch for a crowd. This recipe serves six; either make it in a shallow 3½-pint (2-litre) dish, or for a party of twelve use two 9-inch (22.5-cm) square foil dishes. These are easy to portion and if you want to freeze them, they couldn't be better. Freeze when assembled in layers, then thaw thoroughly before cooking in the normal way. When buying the lasagne choose a thin lasagne sheet. Barilla pre-cooked lasagne is best.

Meat sauce
1 lb (450 g) raw minced beef
2 oz (50 g) bacon pieces, chopped
8 oz (225 g) onion, chopped
6 sticks celery, chopped
1 oz (25 g) flour
½ pint (300 ml) water
3½ oz (90 g) can tomato purée
8 oz (227 g) can peeled tomatoes
2 fat cloves garlic, crushed
1 tablespoon redcurrant jelly
1 beef stock cube
1 teaspoon salt
freshly ground black pepper
good pinch mixed dried herbs

White sauce
1½ oz (40 g) butter
1½ oz (40 g) flour
good pinch ground nutmeg
salt and freshly ground black pepper
1 pint (600 ml) milk
1 level teaspoon Dijon mustard
3 oz (75 g) mature Cheddar cheese, grated
3 oz (75 g) Gruyère cheese, grated

about 6 oz (175 g) uncooked lasagne
a little grated Parmesan cheese

For the meat: put the beef and bacon in the pan. Heat gently until the fat runs, then increase heat and fry until browned. Add the onion and celery and cook for 5 minutes, stir and then add the remaining ingredients and bring to the boil. Reduce the heat, cover the pan and simmer for about one hour.

For the white sauce: melt the butter in a saucepan and stir in the flour, nutmeg, salt and pepper and cook gently for 2 minutes. Remove the pan from the heat and gradually add the milk, stirring to make a smooth mixture. Return the pan to the heat and cook, stirring until the sauce has thickened. Add mustard and check seasoning. Combine the Cheddar and Gruyère cheese.

In a shallow 3½-pint (2-litre) casserole put a third of the meat sauce, the white sauce and a third of the cheese, followed by half of the uncooked lasagne (lay edge to edge, not overlapping). This usually takes 3 pieces, but if necessary break to size. Then start again with a third of the meat sauce, white sauce and cheese, and the remaining lasagne. Repeat, finishing with a final layer of meat sauce, white sauce and cheese and the grated Parmesan. Leave to become cold.

Heat the oven to 350F (180C) gas 4.

Cook the lasagne for about 45 minutes to one hour or until the top is brown and bubbling. Serve at once or keep warm at 200F (100C) gas for up to one hour if necessary.

Serves 6

SAVOURY STUFFED PANCAKES

All that is needed is a green salad and perhaps some French bread for a Sunday lunch with a difference.

Batter
4 oz (100 g) plain flour
1 egg
¼ pint (150 ml) milk
¼ pint (150 ml) water
1 tablespoon corn or vegetable oil
oil for frying

Filling
10.6 oz (300 g) packet frozen leaf spinach
4 oz (100 g) ham, cubed
salt and freshly ground black pepper

Sauce
1 oz (25 g) butter
1 oz (25 g) flour
½ pint (300 ml) milk
3 oz (75 g) Cheddar cheese, grated

Make the batter: measure the flour into a bowl and make a well in the centre. Add the egg and gradually stir in half the milk and water. Blend in the flour from the sides of the bowl and beat well until the mixture is smooth. Stir in the remaining milk, water and oil.

Heat a little oil in an 8-inch (20-cm) frying pan; when hot, pour off the excess oil and spoon about 2 tablespoons of the batter into the pan. Cook the pancake for about one minute until golden brown underneath, then carefully loosen the edges, turn over with a palette knife and cook for a further minute. Turn out and make seven more pancakes in the same way.

Heat the oven to 400F (200C) gas 6.

Now make the filling: cook the spinach as directed on the packet, drain well and add the chopped ham and seasoning and mix well.

Lay the pancakes on a flat work surface and divide the filling

between them. Roll up and lift into a shallow ovenproof dish in a single layer.

Now make the sauce: melt the butter in a small saucepan, add the flour and cook for a minute. Stir in the milk and bring to the boil, stirring until the sauce has thickened; add the cheese and season to taste. Pour this sauce over the pancakes and bake in the oven for about 20 to 25 minutes until hot through.

Serves 4

Egg and Fish Pancakes

7 oz (200 g) can tuna fish, drained and flaked
2 hard-boiled eggs, chopped
10.4-oz (295-g) can condensed mushroom soup
2 tablespoons chopped parsley
8 pancakes
a little melted butter

In a saucepan put the tuna fish, eggs, soup, milk and parsley and heat through until blended. Divide the mixture between the pancakes, roll up and lay in a single layer in an ovenproof dish. Brush with melted butter and bake in the oven as above.

Serves 4

VEGETARIAN PANCAKES

2 oz (50 g) butter
1 large onion, chopped
8 oz (225 g) courgettes, thinly sliced
1 green pepper, chopped
8 oz (225 g) tomatoes, skinned and quartered
salt and pepper

8 pancakes
about 2 oz (50 g) Cheddar cheese, grated

Melt the butter in a saucepan and fry the onion and courgettes until just tender about 5 to 8 minutes. Then add the remaining ingredients except the pancakes and cheese and cook for a further 5 minutes. Taste and check seasoning. Divide the mixture between the pancakes, roll up and arrange in a single layer in an ovenproof dish. Sprinkle with cheese and bake in the oven as above.

Serves 4

Hot Puddings

There's nothing to beat a steaming hot pudding or a crusty apple pie on a cold winter's day, and if you're serving a roast, it's a simple matter to whip up a pudding – especially if you have a blender or processor – and slip it in to take advantage of the oven heat. And it doesn't take long to make one of our traditional English fruity puddings with a crumble topping – I make a habit of storing fruit from the garden as the months go by, ready-sugared, in the freezer. But take my advice and don't leave it until the last minute, or something is bound to happen to stop you and the family will be disappointed, especially if they don't have the opportunity of eating many puddings during the week, and they look forward to it as a Sunday treat.

All our favourites are here from the Old-fashioned treacle tart to the apple and lemon pancakes that are so quickly consumed at our house. (Pancakes freeze well, of course, if made in advance and stored in the freezer between layers of greaseproof paper). I was going to say that most of my hot puddings re-heat well the following day, but there's seldom very much left over.

If you don't have time to make a custard, serve your hot puddings with a good vanilla ice cream, or make 'Danish cream', which my family like: I make up some very thick custard using powder in my blender, then when it has cooled slightly, I stir in an equal quantity of cream – single will do. It makes a rich-tasting alternative to the egg-based custard on page 102.

Apple Pancakes

These pancakes are stuffed ahead, then the parcels are fried in butter just before serving.

Pancake mixture
4 oz (100 g) plain flour
1 egg
½ pint (300 ml) milk and water mixed
1 tablespoon corn or vegetable oil
oil for frying

Filling
4 large Bramley apples, peeled, cored and sliced
¼ teaspoon ground cinnamon
6 oz (175 g) demerara sugar
3 oz (75 g) butter
a little oil for frying

Make the batter: measure the flour into a bowl and make a well in the centre. Add the egg and gradually stir in half the milk and water. Blend in the flour from the sides of the bowl and beat well until the mixture is smooth. Stir in the remaining milk, water and the tablespoon of oil.

Heat a little more oil in an 8-inch (20-cm) frying pan. When hot, pour off the excess oil and spoon about 2 tablespoons of the batter into the pan and swirl it to coat the base. Cook the pancake for about 1 minute until golden-brown underneath. Carefully loosen the edges and turn over with a palette knife and cook for a further minute. Turn out and make 7 more pancakes in the same way.

For the filling: cook the apples in a saucepan with the cinnamon, sugar and butter until tender. This will take about 15 minutes. Remove the pan from the heat and beat the purée well. Spread the pancakes flat, spoon some of the apple mixture on to each and roll them up.

Heat a little oil in a large frying pan and fry the pancakes on all sides until golden brown. Pile on a warm dish and sprinkle with a little extra demerara sugar. Serve with whipped cream.

Serves 4

Lemon Pancakes

Serve plain pancakes with lemon wedges and caster sugar or vanilla sugar.

Banana Pancakes

Slice three bananas and put in a saucepan with 2 oz (50 g) demerara sugar. Cook gently until the sugar has melted. Spoon on to the pancakes, roll up and serve at once with whipped cream.

Serves 4

Bread and Butter Pudding

This family favourite is simple to make, but be sure to let it stand for about an hour before cooking to ensure a light, crisp pudding.

4 oz (100 g) butter
12 slices white bread with the crusts removed
4 oz (100 g) raisins, sultanas and currants
2 oz (50 g) sugar
grated rind of half a lemon
grated rind of half an orange
2 eggs
3/4 pint (450 ml) milk

Butter a 2-pint (a good litre) pie dish.

Butter the slices of bread and cut each in four. Layer the bread in the dish, sprinkling a few raisins between each layer. Sprinkle the remaining raisins over the top with the sugar and grated lemon and orange rind. Beat the eggs and milk together, pour over the bread and leave to stand for about an hour.

Heat the oven to 350F (180C) gas 4, and cook the pudding for 40 minutes until pale golden and firm, serve at once.

Serves 6

RASPBERRY ALMOND CRUMBLE

This is a good way of serving the last of the raspberries with the first of the windfall cooking apples.

Crumble topping
4 oz (100 g) plain flour
2 oz (50 g) ground almonds
3 oz (75 g) margarine
2 oz (50 g) light soft brown sugar

Raspberry filling
12 oz (350 g) cooking apples
12 oz (350 g) raspberries
4 oz (100 g) caster sugar
2 tablespoons water
1 oz (25 g) flaked almonds

Heat the oven to 400F (100C) gas 6.

Put the flour in a bowl with the ground almonds. Add the margarine cut in small pieces and rub in with the fingertips until the mixture resembles breadcrumbs. Stir in the brown sugar.

Peel, core and slice the apples and put in a pie dish with the raspberries, caster sugar and water.

Pile the crumble mixture on top of the fruit, then sprinkle with flaked almonds. Bake for 40 minutes, or until the crumble topping is golden brown and the apples tender. Serve with plenty of thin cream.

Serves 6

Apple and Almond Dessert Cake

I have made this on Sundays for years; it is moist and good, and I can highly recommend it. My husband is not keen on almonds, so I sometimes add the grated rind of a lemon instead of the almond essence and I just sieve a little icing sugar on top before serving, instead of the flaked almonds. Serve warm – you can make it ahead and reheat it. Cream – whipped, pouring or clotted – goes with it well.

5 oz (150 g) butter
2 large eggs
8 oz (225 g) caster sugar
1 teaspoon almond essence
8 oz (225 g) self-raising flour
1½ teaspoons baking powder
12 oz (350 g) cooking apples, weighed after peeling (windfalls do nicely)

Well grease a loose-bottomed 8-inch (20-cm) round cake tin, or an 8-inch (20-cm) springform mould.

Melt the butter in a saucepan over medium heat, without allowing the butter to colour, and pour it into a roomy mixing bowl. Add the eggs, caster sugar and almond essence. Beat well until mixed. Fold in the flour and baking powder. Spread just under two-thirds of the mixture in the tin. Straight away peel, core and slice the apples and arrange them fairly evenly on top of the mixture in the tin. Drop the remaining cake mixture on top of the apples in random dollops – it won't spread. This is not easy as it tends to stick to the apples.

Bake at 350F (180C) gas 4, for about 1½ hours. If the top gets too brown, lower the oven temperature to 325F (160C) gas 3, towards the end of the cooking time. The top should be pale brown, the apple tender when prodded with a warm skewer. Carefully loosen round the sides of the cake with a knife, then push the cake out. If using a springform tin, loosen the cake, then undo the clip and remove the sides.

Dust with a generous layer of sieved icing sugar.

Serves 6 to 8

SPOTTED DICK

Traditionally, Spotted Dick was boiled in a cloth. I find it far easier to make it in a pudding basin. You could perhaps steam it on top of boiled beef and carrots. Serve with syrup sauce and if 'they' demand it, custard too!

4 oz (100 g) self-raising flour
4 oz (100 g) fresh white breadcrumbs
4 oz (100 g) shredded suet
2 oz (50 g) caster sugar
6 oz (175 g) currants
finely greated rind of 1 lemon
about ¼ pint (150 ml) milk

Put the flour, breadcrumbs, suet, sugar, currants and lemon rind in a bowl and mix well, then add sufficient milk to make a medium dropping consistency. Well grease a 1½-pint (900-ml) pudding basin and put in the mixture. Cover with a piece of greased greaseproof paper with a pleat in the centre, to allow for rising, and cover with foil.

Steam or boil for 2 to 3 hours. If boiling, place on an upturned saucer in a saucepan with boiling water coming half-way up the sides of the basin. In either case, keep an eye on the water level and top up with boiling water during cooking if necessary.

Remove the lids, turn out on to a warmed plate and serve with a hot sauce made with the juice from the lemon, 8 tablespoons golden syrup and two tablespoons hot water, blended together.

Serves 6

BUTTERSCOTCH SAUCY PUDDING

A delicious pudding with a rich creamy sauce.

4 oz (100 g) muscovado sugar
4 oz (100 g) soft margarine
2 eggs
6 oz (175 g) self-raising flour
1 level teaspoon baking powder
5 tablespoons milk

Topping
3 oz (75 g) butter
5 oz muscovado sugar
4 tablespoons double cream

Heat the oven to 350F (180C) gas 4. Lightly butter a shallow 2½-pint (1.5-litre) ovenproof dish.

Using the all-in-one method of cake-making, prepare the sponge base. In a large bowl put the sugar, margarine, eggs, flour, baking powder and milk; beat well for about 2 minutes until smooth. Turn into the dish and smooth the top. Bake for about an hour until well-risen and golden brown.

Now prepare the sauce: melt the butter in a saucepan, then add the sugar and cream and mix well. Bring to the boil and simmer gently for 3 minutes, stirring occasionally until thick and glossy. Pour this sauce over the sponge and place the dish under a hot grill for about 2 minutes until the sauce begins to bubble, then serve at once.

Serves 6 to 8

APPLE CHARLOTTE

This is especially popular with grown-ups who, from time to time, like proper puddings. Make it in the early autumn when apples are plentiful – windfalls would be ideal.

about 12 slices thin white bread from a large loaf
6 oz (175 g) butter
3 lb (1.3 kg) cooking apples
6 oz (175 g) light soft brown sugar or demerara sugar
4 tablespoons water

Heat the oven to 400F (200C) gas 6, and butter a shallow 3½-pint (2-litre) ovenproof dish. Spread the bread thinly with butter on one side with a 2-inch (5-cm) cutter, stamp out four rounds from each slice of bread. Arrange the bread over the sides and base of the dish, reserving a few circles for the top.

Peel, core and slice the apples and place in a saucepan with the sugar and water. Cover and cook gently until soft and thick, then beat with a wooden spoon until smooth. Spoon into the dish and cover the top with the remaining circles of bread. Sprinkle the top with a little extra brown sugar and bake for 25 to 30 minutes until the bread is crisp and golden brown. Serve piping hot with thin cream or ice cream.

Serves 8

Pears in Cream

Very good! This quantity is for four, but it is very easy to double-up for a larger gathering. It needs to be done at the last minute, or left to cook whilst eating the main course.

4 pears
2 oz (50 g) butter
¼ pint (150 ml) double cream
a little light soft brown sugar

Heat the oven to 350F (180C) gas 4.

Peel, core and neatly slice the pears. Heat the butter in a frying pan and fry the pears for about 10 minutes or until just tender, without letting them brown. Turn into an ovenproof serving dish. Pour over the cream and bake in the oven for about 15 to 20 minutes, when the cream will have thickened slightly.

Remove from the oven, sprinkle with a little light soft brown sugar and serve at once.

Serves 4

PINEAPPLE MERINGUE PUDDING

This pudding can be served hot or cold and is sure to be a favourite with all the family.

15-oz (425-g) can pineapple pieces
about ¾ pint (450 ml) milk
2 oz (50 g) butter
3 oz (75 g) caster sugar
2 eggs, separated
2 oz (50 g) plain flour

Heat the oven to 300F (150C) gas 2. Butter a shallow 2-pint (a good litre) ovenproof dish.

Drain the pineapple and reserve the syrup. Put the pineapple in the dish and make the syrup up to 1 pint (600 ml) with milk.

In a saucepan, cream the butter and 1 oz (25 g) of the caster sugar until light, then blend in the egg yolks, flour and liquid and bring to the boil, stirring continuously until thickened. Pour at once on to the pineapple.

Whisk the egg whites, using a rotary or electric hand whisk until stiff, then whisk in the remaining sugar a teaspoonful at a time. Spoon over the pineapple custard, making sure that the meringue is spread right out to the edges of the dish.

Cook in the oven for 15 to 20 minutes until the meringue is tinged golden brown. Serve hot or cold.

Serves 4 to 6

SWISS BAKED ALASKA

A great favourite with children.

1 Swiss roll, cut into eight slices
1 brick of strawberry ice cream

Meringue
3 egg whites
6 oz (175 g) caster sugar

Arrange the slices of Swiss roll close together on an ovenproof plate or dish.

Keep the ice cream very cold.

Now make the meringue: whisk the egg whites with an electric or hand whisk until very stiff, then whisk in the sugar a teaspoonful at a time.

Heat the oven to 425F (220C) gas 7.

When the oven is up to temperature, place the ice cream on top of the Swiss roll and mask entirely with the meringue, making sure that it is completely covered.

Put in the oven for just 3 minutes so that the meringue is tinged a pale golden brown.

Serve at once so that the ice cream is still hard under the warm meringue.

Serves 6

RASPBERRY BAKEWELL

Try this with other fruits such as plums, apricots or rhubarb

Pastry
6 oz (175 g) plain flour
1½ oz (40 g) margarine
1½ oz (40 g) lard
about 6 teaspoons cold water

Filling
4 oz (100 g) butter
4 oz (100 g) caster sugar
1 egg, beaten
2 oz (50 g) ground rice
2 oz (50 g) ground almonds
8 oz (225 g) raspberries

Make the pastry: put the flour in a bowl, add fats cut in small pieces and rub in with the fingertips until the mixture resembles fine bread-crumbs. Add sufficient cold water to mix to a firm dough. Roll out the pastry on a floured surface and use to line an 8-inch (20-cm) fluted flan ring on a baking sheet. Prick the base of the flan with a fork and leave to rest in the refrigerator for 10 minutes, whilst making the filling.

Heat the oven to 400F (200C) gas 6.

Now make the filling: melt the butter in a small saucepan, remove the pan from the heat, add the sugar and beaten egg and mix well. Stir in the ground rice and almonds.

Put the raspberries in the flan case and spoon over the rest of the filling. Bake for 30 minutes, then remove the flan ring. Return the flan to the oven for a further 15 minutes. The almond mixture will be well risen and golden brown. Serve warm with cream.

Serves 6

TRADITIONAL APPLE Pie

Windfalls will do well for this pie; you can add either cloves or a little lemon rind.

1½ lb (675 g) cooking apples
2 to 3 oz (50 to 75g) caster sugar
4 cloves

Pastry
6 oz (175 g) plain flour
1½ oz (40 g) margarine
1½ oz (40 g) lard
about 6 teaspoons cold water
milk to glaze
granulated sugar

Put a pie funnel in the centre of a 2-pint (a good litre) pie dish. Peel, core and slice the apples thickly, and arrange half in the pie dish. Sprinkle with sugar and arrange the cloves evenly amongst the apple slices; cover with the remaining apple slices and add about 3 tablespoons cold water. Make the pastry as for Raspberry Bakewell (on opposite page), then roll it out and cover the top of the pie dish, using any trimmings to decorate, if liked. Chill for 30 minutes.

Heat the oven to 400F (200C) gas 6.

Brush the pie with a little milk and sprinkle the top with granulated sugar; make a small slit in the centre for the steam to escape.

Bake in the oven for 40 to 45 minutes until the apple is tender and the pastry crisp and golden brown. Serve hot, with cream or ice cream.

Serves 6

Blackberry and Apple Pie

This pie may be made in advance and frozen without cooking the pastry. Cover it with a double thickness of foil. When needed, make two slits in the pastry and cook from frozen for about 10 to 15 minutes longer than usual.

8 oz (225 g) cooking apples, peeled, cored and sliced
4 oz (100 g) blackberries
about 2 oz (50 g) granulated sugar
1 tablespoon water
1 level tablespoon cornflour

Pastry
8 oz (225 g) plain flour
2 oz (50 g) margarine
2 oz (50 g) lard
about 3 tablespoons cold water

Put the apples, blackberries, sugar and water in a saucepan and simmer very gently for about 20 minutes, or until the apple is tender. Blend the cornflour with a little cold water and stir into the fruit. Cook for two minutes, or until the mixture has thickened. Leave to cool.

Meanwhile make the pastry: put the flour in a large bowl, add the fats cut in small pieces and rub in with the fingertips until the mixture resembles fine breadcrumbs. Add the cold water and work to a firm dough. If the fruit has not cooled, wrap the pastry in foil and chill.

Divide the pastry in half, roll out one piece and use to line the base of an 8-inch (20-cm) enamel or foil pie plate. Put the fruit on to the pastry, dampen the edges with a little water. Roll out the remaining pastry and use to cover the pie; crimp the edges together and seal firmly. If not required immediately, cover with a double thickness of foil, label and freeze.

Make two small slits in the top of the pie, brush with a little milk and bake at 425F (220C) gas 7, for about 45 minutes, or until the pastry is golden brown and crisp.

Serves 4–6

Old-fashioned Treacle Tart

This traditional pudding uses golden syrup, not treacle as the recipe suggests! It is a family favourite both with children and adults.

Pastry
4 oz (100 g) plain flour
1 oz (25 g) lard
1 oz (25 g) butter
about one tablespoon cold water

Filling
4 rounded tablespoons golden syrup
2 oz (50 g) fresh white breadcrumbs
grated rind and juice of half a lemon

Heat the oven to 400F (200C) gas 6.

Measure the flour into a bowl, add the fats cut in small pieces and rub in with the fingertips until the mixture resembles fine breadcrumbs. Add sufficient cold water to mix to a firm dough. Roll out the pastry and line a 7-inch (17.5-cm) flan dish. Chill for 5 minutes.

Meanwhile mix together the filling ingredients and pour into the flan case, using pastry trimmings to decorate the top with twisted strips, if liked. Bake for about 25 minutes, until the pastry is golden brown. Serve warm with cream.

Serves 4–6

LEMON MERINGUE PIE

If you want to make this in a white china flan dish it will take longer to bake blind, so lower the oven temperature to 350F (180C) gas 4. When you remove the foil, paper or beans, allow a further 10 minutes for the base to be really cooked through.

Pastry
4 oz (100 g) plain flour
1 oz (25 g) butter
1 oz (25 g) lard
1 egg yolk
1 teaspoon caster sugar
1 teaspoon cold water

Lemon filling
2 large lemons
1½ oz (40 g) cornflour
½ pint (300 ml) water
2 egg yolks
3 oz (75 g) caster sugar

Meringue topping
3 egg whites
5 oz (150 g) caster sugar

First make the pastry: put the flour in a bowl, add the fats, cut into small pieces. Rub in with the fingertips until the mixture resembles fine breadcrumbs. Mix the egg yolk, sugar and water together and stir into the dry ingredients and bind them together. Roll out the pastry on a floured surface and line an 8-inch (20-cm) flan tin. Chill for 30 minutes.

Heat the oven to 425F (220C) gas 7, with a thick baking sheet in it. Line the pastry in the flan tin with foil or greaseproof paper and weigh down with baking beans. Bake blind for 15 minutes, then remove the paper and beans and return the flan to the oven for a further 5 minutes' baking.

Meanwhile prepare the filling: finely grate the rind and squeeze the juice from the lemons. Put grated rind and juice in a bowl with the cornflour; add 2 tablespoons of the water and blend to a smooth paste. Boil the remaining water and pour it on to the cornflour mixture. Return it to the pan, bring to the boil and simmer for 3 minutes until thick, stirring continuously. Remove from the heat and add the egg yolks blended with the sugar; return the pan to the heat for a moment to thicken the sauce and then cool slightly. Spoon into the flan case.

Whisk the egg whites with an electric or rotary whisk until they form stiff peaks, add the sugar a teaspoonful at a time, whisking well after each addition. Spoon the meringue over the lemon filling, being careful to spread it right up to the edge of the pastry, leaving no air spaces. Return the pie to the oven and reduce the heat to 325F (160C) gas 3 for about 30 minutes, or until the meringue turns a pale golden brown. Serve warm.

Serves 6

CUSTARD TART

It is essential with custard tart to bake the pastry case blind first, otherwise the pastry will be soggy.

Pastry
4 oz (100 g) plain flour
1½ oz (40 g) butter
1 oz (25 g) lard
1 egg yolk
½ oz (12½ g) caster sugar
about 1 teaspoon cold water

Custard filling
2 eggs
1 oz (25 g) caster sugar
½ pint (300 ml) milk
a little grated nutmeg

First make the pastry: put the flour in a bowl, add the fats cut in small pieces and rub in with the fingertips until the mixture resembles fine breadcrumbs. Mix the egg yolk with the sugar and water and stir into the pastry crumbs and bind together. Roll out the pastry on a floured surface and line a 7-inch (17.5-cm) flan ring on a baking sheet and chill for 30 minutes.

Heat the oven to 425F (220C) gas 7. Line the flan ring with foil or greaseproof paper and weigh down with a smaller light tin or baking beans and bake blind for 15 minutes.

Meanwhile prepare the custard: beat the eggs and sugar together, then stir in the milk.

Remove the beans, or tin and greaseproof paper or foil, and turn the oven down to 400F (200C) gas 6. If the pastry has cracked, seal with a little beaten egg white. Pour the custard mixture into the flan and sprinkle with nutmeg. Cook in the oven for 15 minutes, then reduce the heat and cook for a further 25 minutes at 350F (180C) gas 4, or until the filling is set. Serve warm on the day it is made.

Serves 4–6

Cold Desserts

It hasn't been an easy task to select the following cold desserts from the very many I've made and tried out on family and friends, but the ones I've chosen do reflect our own preferences. You may gather that we are fond of chocolate, that I like to follow the seasons in the fruit garden – adapting such recipes as Rhubarb 'brûlée' to other suitable fruits such as blackberries – and that we all adore ice cream. I particularly enjoy experimenting with the 'new' fruits and flavours now available. The Passion fruit ice was voted a success and the family are fans of the tangy, juicy, pale green kiwi fruit – especially in fruit salads. When serving ices – as we often do – remember to take them out of the freezer to soften in the refrigerator for half an hour beforehand.

Always be on the look-out for new ways of serving your desserts. I have served rich ices in demi-tasse coffee cups, with crisp thin biscuits in the saucers; wine glasses, too, have been pressed into service for fruit salads and syllabub. Invest in an ice-cream scoop, pile the individual scoops of sorbet in a clear glass bowl and cover with cling film in the coldest part of the refrigerator until ready to serve.

Two things I would never be without – my vanilla sugar (the children love it on pancakes) and lemons – so good for 'correcting' an over-sweet sauce or adding an extra dimension to stewed apple or rhubarb. Buy five or six at a time (they are often cheaper this way) and keep them in a polythene bag in the refrigerator.

One last word: never be afraid to ask a friend for the recipe of something you've enjoyed. After all, it's a compliment to the cook. And be generous with your recipes in turn. A great deal of the pleasure I have gained from developing and testing these recipes is in sharing them with friends.

And our family's Top Three cold desserts? The Chocolate brandy charlotte, the Walnut and coffee cream tart – and the Rather special fresh fruit salad.

BLACKBERRY ICE CREAM

A deliciously different ice cream and very easy to make as it needs no whisking during freezing. A useful recipe for blackberrying time!

1 lb (450 g) blackberries
4 eggs, separated
4 oz (100 g) caster sugar
½ pint (300 ml) double cream

Reduce the blackberries to a purée in a blender or processor and then sieve to remove all the pips.

Whisk the egg yolks in a small bowl until blended. In a larger bowl whisk the egg whites until stiff, then whisk in the sugar a teaspoonful at a time. The egg whites will get stiffer as the sugar is added. Blend in the yolks until no streaks of colour remain.

Whisk the cream until it forms soft peaks, then fold it into the egg mixture with the fruit purée until well blended.

Turn into a 2½-pint (1.4-litre) container. Cover, label and freeze until solid. Leave to thaw at room temperature for about 10 minutes before serving.

Serves 8 to 10

Passion Fruit Ice Cream

This subtly flavoured ice cream is delicious and refreshing.

6 passion fruit
4 eggs, separated
4 oz (100 g) caster sugar
½ pint (300 ml) double cream

Cut the passion fruit in half and scoop out the pips and flesh. Rub through a sieve to remove the pips.

Whisk the egg yolks in a small bowl until blended. In a larger bowl whisk the egg whites until stiff, then whisk in the sugar a teaspoonful at a time; the egg whites will get stiffer and stiffer as the sugar is added. Blend in the egg yolks until no streaks of colour remain.

Whisk the cream in a small bowl until it forms soft peaks, then fold into the egg mixture with the fruit purée until well mixed. Turn into a 2½-pint (1.4-litre) container. Cover and label and freeze until solid.

Leave to thaw at room temperature for 5 minutes before serving.

Serves 8 to 10

LIME SORBET

A very refreshing finish to a rich meal, especially good on a hot summer Sunday – and it can be made well in advance.

6 limes
½ pint (300 ml) water
6 oz (175 g) sugar
1 egg white
6 sprigs fresh lemon balm, optional

Peel the rind thinly from one lime and put in a small saucepan with the water and sugar. Heat gently until the sugar has dissolved, then simmer for 10 minutes. Strain into a bowl and leave to cool.

Squeeze all the limes and add the juice to the sugar syrup. Cover and freeze until slushy.

Whisk the egg white until stiff, then blend into the partly frozen mixture and return to the freezer to freeze until solid.

Leave to thaw at room temperature for 10 minutes before serving, piled in glasses and decorated with small sprigs of fresh lemon balm.

Serves 6

ST CLEMENT'S MOUSSE

This is very nice served with thin cream and crisp shortbread biscuits.

4 eggs
1 oz (25 g) caster sugar
½ carton frozen orange juice, thawed
juice of half a lemon
½ oz (12½ g) powdered gelatine (1 packet)
3 tablespoons water

Separate the eggs, place the yolks in a bowl with the sugar and whisk until thick and creamy. Add the orange and lemon juice to the egg mixture and mix well. Place the gelatine in a small bowl with the water and leave for 3 minutes until it forms a sponge. Stand the bowl in a pan of simmering water and allow the gelatine to dissolve. Cool slightly, then stir into the orange mixture. Leave for a few minutes until the mixture starts to thicken.

Whisk the egg whites with a hand rotary or electric whisk until stiff and then fold into the orange mixture.

Turn into a 2-pint (1-litre) glass dish and chill until set.

Remove from the refrigerator about 30 minutes before serving.

Serves 4

Coffee Mousse

If the evaporated milk is well chilled, it will give a good volume when whisked and makes a delicious soft mousse.

4 eggs
4 oz (100 g) caster sugar
½ oz (12½ g) powdered gelatine (1 packet)
3 tablespoons water
6 oz (170 g) can evaporated milk, well chilled
2 to 3 tablespoons coffee essence

Separate the eggs and place the yolks in a bowl with the sugar and beat well until creamy. Place the whites in a large bowl, ready for whisking.

Put the gelatine and water in a cup and leave for 3 minutes until it forms a sponge, then stand the cup in a bowl of simmering water and allow the gelatine to dissolve. Remove from the heat and leave to cool slightly.

Meanwhile, whisk the evaporated milk until very thick and about three times the original volume, then whisk the egg whites until stiff and forming soft peaks. Stir the gelatine into the egg yolk mixture with the coffee essence and fold in the evaporated milk and lastly the egg whites.

Turn into a glass serving dish and chill well before serving.

Serves 6

Mocca Suprême

A delicious rich pudding, ideal for adults after a special dinner, although my children will raid the refrigerator and tell me that it is perfect for them too!

½ oz (12½ g) powdered gelatine (1 packet)
2 tablespoons water
2 oz (50 g) chocolate chips (plain chocolate is better than milk chocolate)
2 level tablespoons instant coffee granules
2 tablespoons brandy or rum
4 eggs, separated
4 oz (100 g) caster sugar
½ pint (300 ml) double cream

Place the gelatine in a cup or small bowl with the water and leave to stand for 2 to 3 minutes until it becomes a sponge. Stand the bowl or cup in a pan of gently simmering water until dissolved and clear; then remove from the heat and leave to cool slightly. Place the chocolate chips, coffee and brandy or rum in a bowl and stand it over the pan of simmering water until the chocolate has melted and the coffee is dissolved. Put the egg yolks in a bowl with the sugar and whisk until thick and creamy and then whisk in the warm chocolate mixture and the gelatine and leave on one side until starting to thicken and set.

Whisk the cream until it forms soft peaks and whisk the egg whites with an electric or hand rotary whisk on high speed until stiff.

Fold the cream and the egg whites into the chocolate mixture with a metal spoon until evenly blended, then turn into a glass serving dish and place in a cool place until set.

Serve with a little thin cream poured over.

Serves 6

PINEAPPLE CREAM

Decorate with sprigs of mint, if you have some in the garden.

16-oz (435-g) can pineapple pieces
½ oz (12½ g) powdered gelatine (1 packet)
2 tablespoons water
2 eggs, separated
3 oz (75 g) caster sugar
1 tablespoon lemon juice
¼ pint (150 ml) whipping cream

Drain the pineapple and retain the juice. Finely chop the pineapple pieces, if necessary.

Place the gelatine in a small bowl with the water; leave for about 3 minutes until it forms a sponge. Place the bowl in a pan of hot water and allow the gelatine to dissolve completely. Remove from the pan and allow to cool. In a mixing bowl, whisk the yolks and sugar with a hand rotary or electric whisk until light and creamy. Stir in the pineapple and lemon juice with the gelatine. Leave in a cool place, stirring frequently, until the mixture is beginning to set.

Whisk the cream in a bowl until thick, then gently fold into the pineapple juice mixture with the chopped pineapple.

Whisk the egg whites until they begin to form peaks and fold into the pineapple mixture. Turn into a 2-pint (a good litre) glass serving dish. Chill well before serving.

Serves 6

ORANGE GLORY

An orange mousse topped with cream and chocolate.

2 teaspoons powdered gelatine
2 tablespoons water
3 eggs, separated
2 oz (50 g) caster sguar
finely grated rind and juice of one orange
2 tablespoons apricot jam
¼ pint (150 ml) whipping cream, whipped
grated chocolate, to decorate

Place the gelatine in a small bowl with the water; leave for about 3 minutes until it forms a sponge. Place the bowl in a pan of hot water and allow the gelatine to dissolve completely. Remove from the pan and allow to cool. Take a mixing bowl, whisk the egg yolks and sugar with a rotary or small electric hand whisk until light and creamy. Stir in the dissolved gelatine, orange rind and juice. Leave in a cool place, stirring frequently, until just beginning to set.

Whisk the egg whites until they just form peaks and then carefully fold into the orange mixture and turn into a 2-pint (a good litre) glass serving dish. Chill in the refrigerator until firm, then spread the jam on top of the mousse. Cover with whipped cream and sprinkle with grated chocolate.

Serves 6

Blackberry Fool

Blackberries are for those of us who live in the country or have them in the garden. They freeze superbly without any effort, just pack into a plastic container and freeze until firm. No need to thaw before cooking, just take care that they don't catch!

1 lb (450 g) blackberries
1 tablespoon lemon juice
4 oz (100 g) light soft brown sugar
¼ pint (150 ml) carton natural yogurt
¼ pint (150 ml) whipping cream

Stew the blackberries slowly in a covered pan with the lemon juice until soft and pulpy; this will take about 15 minutes. Add the sugar and stir with a wooden spoon until dissolved.

Purée in a blender or processor until smooth, then sieve into a bowl in order to remove all the seeds. Leave to cool slightly, then stir in the yogurt. Lightly whisk the cream until it forms soft peaks, then fold into the blackberry purée, using a metal spoon.

Turn into a glass serving dish and chill overnight before serving.

Serves 4 to 6

ZABAGLIONE

A simple recipe that needs to be eaten as soon as it is made.

6 tablespoons Marsala or Madeira
4 oz (100 g) caster sugar
4 egg yolks

Stand an ovenglass bowl over a pan of simmering water. Measure the wine and sugar into the bowl and leave to get really warm, but not hot. Add the yolks and at once begin whisking and continue whisking until light and foamy. Pour into four large, stemmed glasses, preferably with a wide brim. Serve at once with thin sweet biscuits.

Serves 4

SYLLABUB WITH KIWI FRUIT

A very rich pudding, but easy to make. It may be made the day before as it keeps well. Serve in individual glasses or glass dishes lined with kiwi fruit.

1 large lemon
4 tablespoons fairly sweet sherry
2 tablespoons brandy
2 oz (50 g) caster sugar
½ pint (300 ml) double cream
2 kiwi fruit

Squeeze the juice from the lemon and put in a bowl with the sherry and brandy. Add the sugar and stir until dissolved. Pour in the cream and whisk until the mixture forms soft peaks. Leave in a cool place until required.

Peel and slice the kiwi fruit. Line each glass or dish with the slices of kiwi fruit, then spoon in the syllabub.

Serves 4

Chocolate Juliette

Make this in advance and leave overnight in the refrigerator so that it sets very firm. Serve cut in thin slices as it is very rich.

7 oz (200 g) bar of milk chocolate
8 oz (225 g) hard margarine
2 eggs
1 oz (25 g) caster sugar
1 oz (25 g) raisins
1 oz (25 g) glacé cherries, quartered
1 oz (25 g) walnuts, chopped
8 oz (225 g) Nice biscuits
¼ pint (150 ml) double cream, whipped
chocolate buttons

Line a small loaf tin 7½ inches (19 cm) by 4 inches (10 cm) by 2½ inches (6 cm) with foil.

Break the chocolate into small pieces and place in a pan with the margarine. Heat gently until melted. Beat the eggs and sugar together until blended, then gradually add the chocolate mixture a little at a time. Stir in the raisins, cherries and nuts.

Break the biscuits into ½-inch (1.25-cm) pieces and stir into the chocolate mixture. Pack into the tin and smooth the top. Leave to set in the refrigerator overnight.

Turn out on to a serving dish and peel off the foil. Decorate with whipped cream and chocolate buttons.

Serves 8 to 10

Rather a Special Chocolate Dessert Cake

I am frequently reminded by my mother that the best chocolate cake she knows is one I did for *Housewife* magazine nearly 20 years ago. So here it is again.

Cake
4 eggs
4 oz (100 g) caster sugar
3 oz (75 g) self-raising flour
1 oz (25 g) cocoa
3 tablespoons vegetable oil

Filling
1/4 pint (150 ml) double cream, whipped
2 tablespoons brandy
1 oz (25 g) caster sugar

Topping
3 oz (75 g) plain chocolate
1 tablespoon brandy
3 tablespoons evaporated milk
5 chocolate flakes cut in half, to decorate

Heat the oven to 350F (180C) gas 4. Line the base of two 8-inch (20-cm) sandwich tins with greased greaseproof paper.

In a large mixing bowl, whisk the eggs and sugar with a rotary or small electric hand whisk until pale and thick enough to leave a trail. Sift the flour and cocoa and carefully fold into the mixture, taking care not to flatten the bulk; stir in the oil. Divide the mixture between the tins, spread out evenly and bake for about 30 minutes until well risen and firm to the touch. Turn out and leave to cool on a wire rack.

In a bowl, whisk the cream, brandy and sugar together until thick and use to sandwich the cakes together.

For the topping: place the chocolate, broken in small pieces with the brandy and evaporated milk, in a bowl over a pan of hot water and allow the chocolate to melt slowly. Once the chocolate has melted, remove from the heat and stir the mixture continuously until thick enough to coat the back of the spoon. Spread over the top of the cake and decorate with the chocolate flakes.

Serves 8 to 10

Chocolate Meringue Gâteau

Make this the day before it is required, as it really does improve with keeping.

3 egg whites
6 oz (175 g) caster sugar

Chocolate filling
¼ pint (150 ml) milk
2 oz (50 g) caster sugar
2 oz (50 g) plain chocolate, broken into small pieces
3 egg yolks
1 level teaspoon cornflour
6 oz (175 g) unsalted butter, softened

Topping
¼ pint (150 ml) double cream, stiffly whipped
12 Maltesers or chocolate buttons

Heat the oven to 300F (150C) gas 2, and line two large baking sheets with non-stick silicone paper.

Put the egg whites in a large bowl and whisk with a hand rotary or an electric whisk until stiff. Gradually whisk in the sugar a teaspoonful at a time. Spread the meringue in two circles 8-inches (20-cm) in diameter on the baking sheets and bake for an hour, then turn off the heat and leave in the oven to cool.

For the chocolate filling: first make the chocolate custard sauce. Put the milk, sugar and chocolate in a basin and place over a pan of hot water. Heat gently until the chocolate has melted and blended with the milk. Stir a little of the hot liquid on to the egg yolks blended with the cornflour, then add to the remaining chocolate mixture and stir until thickened. This will take about 5 to 10 minutes and is ready when the sauce will coat the back of the spoon. Remove from the heat and leave to become quite cold.

Cream the butter and beat in the chocolate sauce. If by any chance the butter cream should curdle because the butter and chocolate are not at the same temperature, warm the bowl slightly by standing in hot water and then beat well. Spread half the chocolate cream on one meringue layer, then cover with the other meringue. Lift on to a flat serving dish, then spread the remaining chocolate cream over the top and swirl into a pattern with a palette knife.

For the topping, pipe 12 large rosettes of cream around the edge of the gâteau. Place a Malteser or chocolate button in the centre of each rosette. Keep in the refrigerator until required, and allow to stand at room temperature for 2 to 3 hours before serving.

Serves 6

CHOCOLATE BRANDY CHARLOTTE

A truly gorgeous chocolate confection: sponge fingers steeped in brandy with a very easy rich chocolate mousse in the centre. The first time I tried it, Bumble – our dog – when little more than a puppy, stole almost half of the charlotte and afterwards slept all afternoon! I've learn my lesson and now such delicious things are put well out of his reach!

Charlotte
about 2 tablespoons brandy
about 2 tablespoons water
1 level tablespoon caster sugar
about 27 sponge fingers

Mousse
4 oz (3.5 g) bar plain chocolate
2 tablespoons water
6 oz (175 g) soft butter
5 oz (150 g) caster sugar
4 eggs, separated

Line a 2-lb (900-g) loaf tin with foil.

Mix the brandy, water and sugar together in a flattish soup plate. Dip each sponge finger, sugar side down into the brandy mixture and arrange 9 or 10, sugar side down, along the base of the tin. Cut the remainder in half and dip in the brandy mixture and stand up all the way around the tin.

To make the mousse: put the chocolate and water in a bowl over a pan of hot water and allow to melt slowly. Cream the butter, sugar and egg yolks together until creamy and then stir in the melted chocolate, this should be just warm, not hot.

Whisk the egg whites until stiff, using a rotary or electric hand whisk, and fold into the chocolate mixture. Turn into the loaf tin and then leave in the refrigerator overnight.

Turn out on to a serving dish, peel off the foil and decorate as liked.

Serves 8, as it is very rich

Walnut and Coffee Cream Tart

Very easy and very rich: the condensed milk can be cooked in the oven when it's on.

14-oz (397-g) can condensed milk

Biscuit base
2 oz (50 g) butter
4 oz (100 g) Digestive biscuits, crushed
1 oz (25 g) demerara sugar

Topping
¼ pint (150 ml) whipping cream
1 teaspoon instant coffee granules
walnut pieces to decorate

Immerse the unopened can of condensed milk in a pan of boiling water; cover and boil for about 4 hours. Remove the can from the pan and allow to cool before opening.

Now make the biscuit base: in a small saucepan melt the butter, then stir in the biscuit crumbs and the brown sugar. Use to line a 9-inch (22.5-cm) loose-bottomed flan tin, pressing the mixture firmly on to the base and around the sides of the tin. Chill in the refrigerator until firm.

Open the condensed milk and spread over the biscuit base; it will be slightly thickened and have a caramel colour and flavour.

For the topping, lightly whisk the cream until just thick, then stir in the coffee granules. Pipe this over the filling and decorate with pieces of walnut. Chill well and then lift on to a serving plate.

Serves 6

Tarte au Citron

Very French. Crisp pastry with a sharp filling tasting like proper homemade lemon curd, but set like a custard. Best served cold with a bowl of lightly whipped cream.

Shortcrust pastry
2 oz (100 g) plain flour
2 oz (50 g) butter
about 4 teaspoons cold water

Lemon filling
4 eggs
6 oz caster sugar
2 oz (50 g) butter melted
grated rind and juice of 2 lemons

Heat the oven to 425F (220C) gas 7, with a baking tray placed on a shelf just above centre.

Put the flour in a bowl, add the butter cut in small pieces and rub in with the fingertips until the mixture resembles fine breadcrumbs. Add sufficient cold water to mix to a firm dough; knead lightly until smooth and then roll out thinly on a floured surface. Line an 8-inch (20-cm) loose-bottomed flan tin with the pastry and chill. Make a foil shape to line the tin, moulding it around a smaller tin. Place on the baking tray and bake blind for about 12 to 15 minutes until evenly baked, removing the foil for the last 5 minutes. Take from the oven and lower the heat to 350F (180C) gas 4.

While the flan is baking, make the filling. Put all the ingredients except the lemon rind and juice in a bowl and place over a pan of hot water until the butter has melted and the sugar has dissolved, stirring continuously, then add lemon rind and juice. Remove the foil from the flan, pour in the filling and cook in the oven for 25 minutes until set. Remove and leave to cool, then lift out of the flan tin and place on a serving plate.

Serves 6

RATHER SPECIAL FRESH FRUIT SALAD

I am not a great one for making a sugar syrup; I find that it works well to layer the fruits early in the day, or the day, before with caster sugar. Use about 2 oz (50 g) sugar to each prepared 1 lb (450 g) of fruit – or less if you like it very sharp. First prepare all the citrus fruit, then any fruit that might discolour ie. pears, apples or grapes – the cut side can go brown. Blend carefully, but well.

1 grapefruit, peeled and segmented
1 melon, peeled, seeded and cut in cubes
2 green eating apples, cored and sliced
juice of one lemon
6–8 oz (175 g to 225 g) caster sugar
8 oz (225 g) black grapes, halved and seeded
2 kiwi fruit, sliced and peeled
1 mango, peeled and cut in wedges from the stone

Place the fruit in layers in a bowl, sprinkling with lemon juice and sugar between each layer. Continue until all the fruit has been used and finishing with a layer of sugar.

Cover the bowl with a plate or piece of cling film and leave overnight in the refrigerator.

Turn into a glass serving dish, mixing lightly so that all the fruits are blended evenly. Serve with plenty of cream.

Serves 8 to 10

STRAWBERRIES CORDON BLEU

A delicious way to serve raspberries and strawberries.

1 lb (450 g) fresh strawberries
juice of one orange

Sauce
8 oz (225 g) fresh raspberries
4 oz (100 g) icing sugar

Wash and hull the strawberries and cut each in half and place in a glass serving dish. Pour over the orange juice and then cover with cling film and leave in the refrigerator until required.

For the sauce: place the raspberries in an electric blender for a few seconds with the icing sugar and purée until smooth, then sieve into a bowl to remove all the pips. Pour into a sauceboat or small glass dish and leave in a cool place until ready to serve.

Serve the strawberries with a little raspberry sauce spooned over.

Serves 4

SUMMER PUDDING

This needs preparing and soaking overnight before turning out and should be served with lots of cream.

6 to 8 large, fairly thin slices white bread with the crusts removed
8 oz (225 g) rhubarb
8 oz (225 g) black currants
8 oz (25 g) granulated sugar
6 tablespoons water
8 oz (225 g) small strawberries
8 oz (225 g) raspberries

Put one slice of bread on one side for the top and use the remainder to line the base and sides of a 2-pint (a good litre) basin or round dish.

Put the rhubarb, cut in ½-inch (1.25-cm) slices, with the black currants in a saucepan; add the sugar and water and bring to the boil and simmer for a few minutes until barely tender, stirring. Add the strawberries and raspberries and cook for a further minute.

Turn the mixture into the lined dish, place the slice of bread on top and bend over the tops of the bread at the sides towards the centre. Place a saucer on top, pressing down a little until the juices rise to the top of the basin or dish. Leave to soak until cold and then put in the refrigerator overnight.

Turn out just before serving, with generous helpings of cream.

Serves 4 to 6

RHUBARB 'BRÛLÉE'

Try this, too, with fresh sliced strawberries or raspberries. First soak them in a little brandy and sugar for a few hours, keeping them chilled.

½ pint (300 ml) whipping cream
½ pint (300 ml) natural yogurt
8 oz (225 g) cooked early rhubarb
dark soft brown sugar

Lightly whip the cream until it forms soft peaks and then stir in the yogurt. Put a spoonful of the cream and yogurt in the base of four individual glass dishes of ½-pint (300-ml) capacity. Divide the rhubarb equally between the dishes, then top with the rest of the cream mixture and smooth flat.

Sprinkle the dishes with a ¼-inch (0.60-cm) layer of sugar. Leave in the refrigerator for several hours.

Sprinkle again with more sugar just before serving.

Serves 4

Hazelnut and Apricot Meringue Cake

4 oz (100 g) hazelnuts
4 egg whites
8 oz (225 g) caster sugar
1 teaspoon white vinegar
15 oz (425 g) can apricot halves
1 rounded teaspoon arrowroot
¼ pint (150 ml) whipping cream

Heat the oven to 375F (190C) gas 5. Lightly brush the sides of two 8-inch (20-cm) sandwich tins with oil and line the bases with a circle of non-stick parchment.

Place the hazelnuts on a tray and put in the oven for a few minutes; tip on to a clean teatowel, then rub them together and the skins should flake off easily. Place the nuts in a blender or processor and grind.

Whisk the egg whites with an electric or hand rotary whisk on high speed until stiff, then whisk in half the sugar a teaspoonful at a time. Mix the remaining sugar with the hazelnuts, then fold this mixture into the egg whites with the vinegar. Divide the mixture between the tins, smooth flat, and bake for 35 minutes, when the meringue will be a pale brown. Turn off the oven and leave the meringues to cool in the oven.

When cold, remove from tins and peel off parchment. Drain apricots, keeping 8 halves aside. Chop the remainder.

Place the arrowroot in a small saucepan and stir in the apricot syrup; place over a moderate heat and cook gently, stirring continuously until thickened. Simmer for a minute or two and then remove from the heat; stir in the chopped apricots and leave to cool.

Whisk the cream until thick. Place one of the meringue cakes on a serving dish and spread with half the cream, then cover with the chopped apricots and top with the remaining meringue cake.

Pipe remaining cream in eight swirls around the edge; decorate the top with the apricot halves. Leave for about an hour before serving.

Serves 8

LEMON AND STRAWBERRY CREAM FLAN

This, I would say, is about the quickest and easiest flan there is! My family adore it and it makes the first strawberries stretch for a taste for everyone.

Flan case
2 oz (50 g) butter
1 level tablespoon demerara sugar
4 oz (100 g) Digestive biscuits, crushed

Filling
14-oz (397-g) can condensed milk
¼ pint (150 ml) double cream
juice of 2 really large lemons
about 4 oz (100 g) halved strawberries

Melt the butter in a saucepan, remove from the heat and stir in the sugar and crushed biscuits. Mix well and press the mixture over the base and sides of an 8 to 9-inch (20 to 22.5-cm) flan ring or loose-bottomed flan tin. Spready evenly using a metal tablespoon.

Put the condensed milk, cream and lemon juice in a bowl and whisk the mixture together until well blended. Pour into the flan case.

Chill for at least four hours in the refrigerator.

Before serving, remove the flan ring and decorate the flan with the halved strawberries.

Serves 6 to 8

Ann's Cream Cheesecake

This cheesecake has no crust or pastry base. It is very rich and creamy and goes well with fresh strawberries or raspberries.

1 lb (450 g) full fat cream cheese, such as Philadelphia
3 eggs
5 oz (150 g) caster sugar
½ teaspoon almond essence
½ pint (300 ml) soured cream
1 teaspoon vanilla essence

Heat the oven to 350F (180C) gas 4.

Put the cream cheese, eggs, sugar and almond essence in a bowl and beat together until smooth, thick and lemon-coloured. Pour into a greased 10-inch (25-cm) pie plate and bake for 25 minutes, then remove from the oven and leave to cool for 20 minutes.

Meanwhile, beat the soured cream with an extra tablespoonful of caster sugar and the vanilla essence until well blended. Pour over the top of the cheesecake, return it to the oven and bake for a further 10 minutes.

Remove from the oven and leave to become quite cold before serving.

Serves 8

FLUFFY PINEAPPLE PIE

This is a very light pineapple mixture served in a biscuit crust. It could be served on its own without the crust in individual dishes.

Flan case
3 oz (75 g) butter
1 oz (25 g) demerara sugar
6 oz (175 g) Digestive biscuits, crushed

Filling
2 tablespoons water
½ oz (12½ g) powdered gelatine (1 packet)
3 eggs, separated
5 oz (150 g) caster sugar
grated rind and juice of 1 lemon
8 oz (225 g) full-fat cream cheese
12-oz (376-g) can crushed pineapple

Melt the butter in a saucepan, stir in the sugar, then remove from the heat and stir in the crushed biscuits. Mix thoroughly. Press the mixture over the base and sides of a 9 to 10-inch (22.5 to 25-cm) fluted loose-bottomed flan tin, using a metal spoon.

Put the water and gelatine in a small cup or bowl and leave to stand for a few minutes to sponge, then stand in a pan of gently simmering water until dissolved. Remove from heat and cool slightly.

Put the egg yolks in a small saucepan with 2 oz (50 g) of the sugar and the lemon rind and juice and mix well with a wooden spoon. Cook over a moderate heat until thickened but not boiled. Take from heat.

Put the cream cheese in a large bowl and beat in the pineapple until well mixed, then stir in the gelatine and egg mixture. Mix thoroughly and leave in a cool place until starting to set.

Whisk the egg whites until stiff, using an electric whisk or hand rotary whisk on high speed, then whisk in the remaining sugar a teaspoonful at a time. Fold the egg whites into the pineapple mixture and pile into the flan case. Leave in a cool place until set.

Serves 8 to 10

Strawberry Cream Roll

This is another way of making a few strawberries go a long way; you could use raspberries too. It is ideal for those unexpected guests.

Swiss roll
3 size 2 eggs, at room temperature
3 oz (75 g) caster sugar, warmed
3 oz (75 g) self-raising flour

Filling
¼ pint (150 ml) double cream
4 oz (100 g) strawberries, sliced
a little caster or vanilla sugar to taste

Heat the oven to 425F (220C) gas 7, and grease and line a Swiss roll tin, 13 × 9 inches (32.5 × 22.5 cm) with greased greaseproof paper. Whisk the eggs and sugar together in a large bowl until the mixture is light and creamy and the whisk will leave a trail when lifted out. Sift the flour and carefully fold it into the mixture with a metal spoon. Turn into the tin and give a gentle shake, or smooth level with the back of the spoon, so that the mixture will find its own level, taking care that it is evenly spread into the corners.

Bake for about 10 minutes until golden brown and the sponge begins to shrink from the edges of the tin.

While the cake is cooking, cut out a piece of greaseproof paper a little bigger than the tin and sprinkle with caster sugar. Invert the cake on to the paper and quickly loosen the paper on the base of the cake and peel off. To make rolling easier, trim all four edges of the sponge and score a line 1 inch (2.5 cm) in from the rolling edge, being careful not to cut through. Roll up the sponge and leave to cool.

Meanwhile, whisk the cream until it forms soft peaks and fold in the sliced strawberries. Add a little caster or vanilla sugar to the cream.

When the sponge is cold, carefully unroll and spread with the strawberry cream; roll up again and place on a serving dish. Leave in a cool place until required. Sprinkle with a little extra caster sugar.

Serves 8

ALMOND BISCUITS

Serve these very thin biscuits with ice cream, fruit salad or syllabub.

3 oz (75 g) butter
3 oz (75 g) caster sugar
2 oz (50 g) plain flour
3 oz (75 g) shredded almonds

Heat the oven to 400F (200C) gas 6. Well butter 3 to 4 baking trays.

Cream the butter and sugar together until light and fluffy, then work in the flour with the almonds

Put the mixture in teaspoons well-spaced on the baking trays, as they spread, and flatten well with a wet fork.

Bake the biscuits for about 8 minutes, until just coloured around the edges.

Remove from the oven and leave to cool for a few minutes before lifting from the tray on to a wire rack to finish cooling.

Store in an air-tight tin until required.

Makes about 24

Index